Menander
and the
Making of Comedy

MENANDER
AND THE
MAKING OF COMEDY

J. MICHAEL WALTON
and
PETER D. ARNOTT

PRAEGER

Westport, Connecticut
London

**The Library of Congress has cataloged the hardcover edition
as follows:**

Walton, J. Michael.
    Menander and the making of comedy / J. Michael Walton and Peter D.
Arnott.
        p.   cm.—(Contributions in drama and theatre studies, ISSN
0163–3821 ; no. 67) (Lives of the theatre)
    Includes bibliographical references and index.
    ISBN 0–313–27216–6 (alk. paper)
    1. Menander, of Athens—Criticism and interpretation. 2. Greek
drama (Comedy)—History and criticism. I. Arnott, Peter D.
II. Title. III. Series. IV. Series: Lives of the theatre.
PA4247.W33   1996
882'.01—dc20   95–38653

British Library Cataloguing in Publication Data is available.

A hardcover edition of *Menander and the Making of Comedy* is available
from Greenwood Press, an imprint of Greenwood Publishing Group, Inc.
(Contributions in Drama and Theatre Studies, Number 67 (Lives of the Theatre);
ISBN 0–313–27216–6).

Library of Congress Catalog Card Number: 95–38653
ISBN: 0–275–93420–9 (pbk.)

First published in 1996

Praeger Publishers, 88 Post Road West, Westport, CT 06881
An imprint of Greenwood Publishing Group, Inc.

Printed in the United States of America

The paper used in this book complies with the
Permanent Paper Standard issued by the National
Information Standards Organization (Z39.48–1984).

10 9 8 7 6 5 4 3 2 1

for Eva and Jennifer Arnott

Contents

Photographs follow page 72

Foreword

This book stems from the Greenwood Press series *Lives of the Theatre*. To facilitate use in college and university courses, some volumes have been selected to appear in paperback. This is such a volume. *Lives of the Theatre* is designed to provide scholarly introductions to important periods and movements in the history of world theatre from the earliest instances of recorded performance through to the twentieth century, viewing the theatre consistently through the lives of representative theatrical practitioners. Although many of the volumes will be centered on playwrights, other important theatre people, such as actors and directors, will also be prominent in the series. The subjects have been chosen not simply for their individual importance, but because their lives in the theatre can well serve to provide a major perspective on the theatrical trends of their eras. They are therefore either representative of their time, figures whom their contemporaries recognized as vital presences in the theatre, or they are people whose work had a fundamental influence on the development of theatre, not only in their lifetimes but after their deaths as well. While the discussion of verbal and written scripts will inevitably be a central concern in any volume that is about an artist who wrote for the theatre, these scripts will always be considered in their function as a basis for performance.

The rubric "Lives of the Theatre" is therefore intended to suggest biographies both of people who created theatre as an institution and as a medium of performance and of the life of the theatre itself. This dual focus will be illustrated through the titles of the individual volumes, such as *Christopher Marlowe and the Renaissance of Tragedy*, *George Bernard Shaw and the Socialist Theatre*, and *Richard Wagner and Festival Theatre*, to name just a few. At the same time, although the focus of each volume will be different, depending on the particular subject, appropriate emphasis will be given to the cultural and political context within which the theatre of any given time is set. Theatre itself can be seen to have a palpable effect on the social world around it, as it both reflects the life of its time and helps to form that life by feeding it images, epitomes, and alternative versions of itself. Hence, we hope that this series will also contribute to understanding the broader social life of the period of which the theatre represented in each volume was a part.

Lives of the Theatre grew out of an idea that Josh Beer put to Christopher Innes and Peter Arnott. Sadly, Peter did not live to see the inauguration of the series. Simon Williams kindly agreed to replace him as one of the series' editors and has played a full part in its preparation. In commemoration, the editors wish to acknowledge Peter's own rich contribution to the life of the theatre.

Josh Beer
Christopher Innes
Simon Williams

Preface

When Peter Arnott died on November 3, 1990, it was in the middle of a teaching term in which he had, as usual, been fully involved. Only forty-eight hours earlier he had given a lecture, two, in fact. He was full of plans for new productions and new books to add to the twenty-five or so he had already published. One of these was a book on Menander, commissioned by Greenwood as one of the inaugural volumes of a new series with the working title of *Lives in the Theatre*.

Peter's widow, Eva, wrote to me the following year inviting me to look at what Peter had already written with a view to completion. I was both flattered and daunted but especially pleased, as Peter's translation of *Hecuba* was to be published that year in *Euripides: Plays Two*, which I had edited. We dedicated the volume to him.

His Menander consisted of an outline plan; several pages of detailed notes; and a handwritten draft of sixty-seven pages, very much a first draft, but recognizable, as in the trireme analogy of the present Chapter 3, as possessing Peter's personal touch. This material forms the basis of the first two chapters of the present book, somewhat revised and reordered to meet the demands of the series and to place more emphasis on Menander in his own time. His section on the influence of Euripides on New Comedy and the recovery of manuscripts has been expanded.

Peter's comprehensive grasp in other areas was an enormous help in assessing priorities for all the later chapters. I hope that he would have approved of the changes I have made, as well as the additions and original material. I know he would have said that he did. He was a generous man for whose help and advice in my own career I remain deeply indebted. As a visitor to the Drama Department in Hull many years ago, when it was still in its comparative infancy, he amazed staff and students by giving one of his flawless, apparently off-the-cuff lectures, without recourse to a single note. That evening with his marionette theatre he transformed amazement into disbelief when he presented his own translation of Aristophanes' *Birds*, a solo *tour de force* in which he manipulated and provided the voices for seventeen characters and a chorus.

It was, of course, this capacity to function as both scholar and practitioner that gave Peter the position of esteem that he enjoyed in the worlds of both theatrical and classical scholarship. He understood the history of the theatre as well as its nuts and bolts. He was the motor engineer as well as the racing driver. Such a rare understanding of the whole craft of the playwright makes it all the sadder that he should have managed to write so little on Menander, a playwright whose pragmatism and subtlety he instinctively appreciated.

Menander, as Peter pointed out, was for so long an absentee from the feast that his eventual arrival was inevitably something of an anticlimax: particularly when the bits turned up piecemeal like the remains of some literary Pentheus, reconstructed by an optimistic Cadmus. By the time we did have a whole play, arguably two, from which to take a more considered position, the rush to judgment had become so Gadarene that the nonspecialist theatre historian was prepared to take it on trust that Menander had been ever so influential in his own time, but that the actual plays were no great loss.

More recent specialist studies into various aspects of Menander's craft have shown that he was far more than an interesting terminus in the history of the drama. The thesis of the present book, if there is one, is that he was a spellbinding story-teller who loved his characters like children, sympathizing with them when they were most unreasonable and doing whatever he could to ensure that they escaped from the scrapes they managed to engineer. "You should always tell stories," wrote that most humane of contemporary novelists John Irving in *The Water Method Man* "in such a way that you make the audience good and wise, even a little ahead of you." It is advice that Menander might have given. It is advice he unwittingly seems to have taken.

Menander was, of course, the product of a period whose tolerance of the restrictions on the lives of most of those about whom he wrote—the poor, women, slaves—renders many of his solutions at best uncomfortable. Any age, we would do well to remember, which takes its own *mores* as the only brand marked "correct" may find itself harshly judged by the tribunal of history. Menander takes society as he finds it. There are no attempts here to change the world, only to value it for the good things while offering consolation for the bad.

In one of his last essays, included here in Appendix 3, Peter Arnott wrote of Menander's *Duskolos* as "one of the great rediscoveries of our time." The professional production of *The Woman from Samos* at the J. Paul Getty Museum in Malibu in October 1994 (see Appendix 4) suggests that this play is another. It is a fitting description, as I hope this book may demonstrate. Parochial as his plays may seem, Menander is the first playwright to appear at home in the modern world. Aeschylus, Sophocles, Euripides, and Aristophanes belong on the world's stages, never more so than in a time as savage as our own and so desperate for means of coming to terms with the major problems that threaten our very existence. Menander reminds us why we bother: why we bother with family, with neighbors, with the business of daily living. When Knemon attempts to abdicate from the human race, he discovers that it is not possible. In the way in which his characters behave toward one another, Menander demonstrates, and demonstrates optimistically, the constancy of human nature.

Wherever possible, the more familiar English or anglicized versions of play titles have been used. I offer my apologies for the inconsistencies this inevitably causes. Translations are my own based on the Oxford Text unless otherwise stated. I also acknowledge the invaluable edition of *Samia* edited by David Bain, (Warminster: Aris and Phillips, 1983). The translations of *The Malcontent* and *The Woman from Samos* are published in *Aristophanes and Menander: New Comedy* (London: Methuen, 1994).

J. Michael Walton
University of Hull

Chapter 1

A Comic Tradition: The Search
for New Comedy

Of all the playwrights who have been sufficiently influential to merit an individual study in a series entitled *Lives of the Theatre*, none can be so shrouded in obscurity as Menander. Little is known about his life, and his work is represented by two almost complete plays and some bits and pieces of a few others. Until the beginning of the twentieth century, indeed, he existed as little more than a name: a famous name certainly, perhaps the most famous lost name of antiquity, but virtually nothing beyond that. Behind such apparent historical modesty lies an improbable story, much of which did not emerge until the present century, two thousand two hundred years after the death of the comic playwright who, above all others, commanded the unquestioning respect of the ancient world. Menander, however, demands attention.

If the details of his career still remain obscure, his significance is defined by the events that surrounded him. Menander was a pivotal figure, presiding over one of the earliest and most important transitional periods in the history of the theatre. If he had not existed, it would have been necessary to invent him, as the Greeks had already half-invented Thespis and Susarion, the legendary founders of tragedy and comedy, respectively.

Menander stood at a point in time when the classical theatre, so rich in the traditions founded and fostered by Aeschylus, Sophocles, Euripides, and Aristophanes, was in danger of following the tide of Athenian history by subsiding gently into nostalgia for its past. Instead, he grabbed hold of the tentative social alternative to political comedy that was beginning to emerge at the time of Aristophanes' death, and that could quite easily have proved a blind alley, and reshaped it as the cornerstone of the subsequent Western comic tradition. His work represents not so much the historic development of an earlier comic form as a fundamental conversion to a new set of priorities. His comedies brought to life the spirit of a new Greek age with all its political, social, and artistic changes. The principles by which he worked were so potent and so universally successful that they virtually obliterated from memory all previous forms of comedy.

FROM OLD TO NEW COMEDY

In the fifth century B.C. the works of Aristophanes dominated the comic stage. They were fierce political and social satires that lampooned institutions and individuals without fear or favor. They were created, as were the later tragedies of Sophocles and Euripides, for an audience under stress and frequently under siege as a result of the Peloponnesian War against Sparta which lasted from 431 until 404 B.C. Aristophanes provided a vivid commentary on the life of the time. The Old Comedies reflect a transition from a carefree, if concerned optimism, as a successful conclusion to the war seems only a matter of time, to an ill-concealed, almost hysterical despair as Athens tries to disguise the impending disaster in a cloak of frenzied gaiety.

In a word, the plays are engaged. They mirror actuality. They are crammed with references drawing attention to the presence of the audience. They serve up the personalities and the events of the day in lampoon style. Although the flood of topicalities and fanciful notions may conceal a serious undercurrent, the mood can be somber and hard-hitting as well as farcical, reflecting anxious times and an anxious audience. Comedy, perhaps, always draws attention to topical neuroses and Menander too will deal in real pain, but Aristophanes has a contemporaneity that persuaded antiquarians that the works were worthy of preservation on purely historical grounds. Aristophanes offers the gossip of the time preserved in amber. He is full of the trivia that more serious sources omit. From Thucydides, the ex-general turned historian, we learn the pattern of the war; we hear the speeches of the elected leaders; we intrude on diplomatic missions; we pursue the failing strategies of battle after battle. From Aristophanes, we learn what it was like to walk down an Athenian street in wartime. We are introduced to the city's real inhabitants, some of whom are so vivid we can almost see them. We hear the grumbles, feel the cold, and learn what it is to be hungry.

This same contemporaneity ensured that Aristophanes' path of comedy was a dramatic cul-de-sac, at least in Athens. There are few jokes as stale as yesterday's satire and in Athens Aristophanes' comedies died with him. Oliver Taplin has recently suggested[1] that performances of Aristophanes' plays may have transcended national boundaries, both in his own time and up to the time when Menander was writing, with regular performances in Sicily and southern Italy. Perhaps they traveled better than anyone has previously assumed. Certainly, extended time has worked to Aristophanes' advantage and a generation of theatre-goers as removed as ours has learned that, although the individual targets might be dead, the types of human folly he pillories span the centuries. The immediate targets may be lost references, but much of the satire is still appropriate. Venal politicians, dumb-struck generals, and demented entrepreneurs are nothing new. Present-day directors have discovered that the finding of a contemporary parallel is not necessarily a better solution than leaving the original targets and letting the audience supply parallels of their own. It was in Athens that Aristophanes seems to have lived only as long as his plays were topical. For reasons that may be in part political, a prismatic view of Athens in 420 B.C. had no market value in the Athens of 380.

If Menander as much as knew of the early plays of Aristophanes, it could only be as museum pieces that he might study as anarchic constructs far removed from his own crafted and crafty plays: with, one might speculate, a sneaking admiration for, and envy of, a time when anything could be said and anything went. The frustration of individual citizens against fumbling bureaucrats and self-seeking politicians was perhaps no less in the Athens of Menander than in that of Aristophanes a hundred years earlier, but the stage had ceased to be a place for its expression. The compensation for Menander was in creating Athenians who were really recognizable, whose problems and concerns were still the stuff of *taverna* gossip but whose expectations of changing the world had been reduced to zero.

In Menander there is a mix of characters, some of whom are comic stereotypes defined by status or profession, but the central figures are what Aristotle might have described as *spoudaios*, "worth taking seriously," however domestic the issues that were exercising their minds and energies. In Aristophanes characters tend to come and go, dramatic mercenaries changeable according to the latest circumstance. They redefine themselves to suit the joke, almost as though the actor's acquired habit of playing so many roles within the same play spilled over into individual characterization. The longer roles, with a few exceptions, seem little more than a series of loosely linked impersonations given a rudimentary continuity by the use of the same name and backed by a restricted range of physical and mental traits. This is the hallmark of an acting tradition that in our present century belongs more to vaudeville or revue than to sustained drama. It is the apogee of masked comedy where the actor is always conscious of an identity as actor, commenting on the performance, exchanging asides with the audience, and assuming a role as one assumes the mask.

Two late plays of Aristophanes, *Ekklesiazousai* (*Women in Assembly* or *Women in Power*, 392 B.C.) and *Ploutos* (*Wealth*, 388 B.C.), written and performed under a less tolerant regime in Athens, seem to suggest that Aristophanes himself may have become aware of a need for a new direction for comedy. *Frogs* (405 B.C.), on the surface a piece of escapist fantasy about bringing a playwright back from the dead, is in essence a last-ditch attempt to salvage anything from a war that is close to its climax. Nothing could be more immediate than Aeschylus' advice to the Athenians to bring back the renegade Alkibiades to salvage their cause: few theatrical stances show more daring, recklessness even, than to castigate the Assembly's decision to condemn six of the generals who fought in a recent and successful sea battle, while enfranchising the slaves who rowed the ships. That was at the Great Dionysia of 405 B.C. The final defeat by the Spartans took place the following year. The great walls from Athens to the Piraeus were pulled down, and the Spartans imposed a tyrannical government. Political comedy died.

It was another thirteen years before *Women in Power*, years that may have seen drama festivals but that have handed down no plays, neither tragedy nor comedy. By 392 much had changed. Performed in a defeated city for an audience that had struggled to survive a postwar financial depression, *Women in Power* and *Wealth* display a marked tendency to avoid topical issues in favor of generalized ones. The subject of *Women in Power* is political, certainly, but confines itself to broad statements about voter apathy and theoretical communism. The play is reminiscent of *Lysistrata* (411 B.C.) in that, once again, it shows women assuming control over the state. There the comparison ends. The women of *Women in Power* disguise themselves as men and vote themselves the authority to create a Utopia in which all things, particularly husbands, are apportioned equally. The humor is mild and non-specific. The particular target, if one can be identified, is current philosophical speculation about the ideal community such as that which infuses Plato's *Republic*. *Women in Power* is a genuinely escapist play, in the spirit, maybe, of the earlier *Festival Time* (*Thesmophoriazousai*, ? 411 B.C.), but shorn of almost all internal reference that could identify its date.

Finally comes *Wealth* in 388 B.C.—Aristophanes was to die some three years later. *Wealth* takes us into the realm of harmless allegory. The title role belongs to the god of wealth, traditionally blind, who has his sight restored through the agency of an Athenian citizen. He thereupon proceeds to distribute his riches, not haphazardly as before but strictly in accordance with merit, thus overturning the accepted patterns of society. *Wealth* ends, as do most Aristophanes plays, with a celebration of the new dispensation, a party that even the gods leave Olympus to join.

Wealth has some enjoyable moments but is on the whole a disappointing epilogue for such an original playwright. The obsession with money reflects the current Athenian situation, and this, if nothing else, might give it a contemporary frisson. Its cynical treatment of the divine hierarchy, represented as abandoning power for wealth, speaks of an age in which the traditional religion was rapidly falling into disrepute. Popular in the Renaissance for its apparently high moral tone, it stands now as a token of the state of Athens in political decline. The Athenians have moved into an age where plays are presented as a diversion and no longer as a nudge to the public conscience, an age that is already beginning to look nostalgically toward the past and one in which the gods, from being regarded as a decisive force in human affairs, have become a literary fabric merely and a convenient source of fairy tales.

Beyond these late works of Aristophanes, we have little clear evidence for the transition from Old Comedy to New. A body of fragments, mostly short and inconclusive, offers something of the flavor of early fourth-century comedy, surfacing as the memory of Aristophanes receded. Some plays, it appears, retained a note of political topicality, but these were in the minority. Where real names were used, they seem to have been drawn from classes of society that could be more safely satirized. The demi-monde provided a gallery of popular characters. The hangers-on who attached themselves to the monied classes, dancing attendance and touting for favors, and whom the Greeks contemptuously called parasites, were rapidly becoming established as regular characters of comedy. Less dangerous victims than the politicians that had provided Aristophanes with targets, they could still be based on known contemporary figures and ridiculed under their own names. By the time of Plautus and Terence, two playwrights who were creating New Comedy in Rome by adapting, a hundred years on, the plays of fourth-century Athens, the parasite had become a stock figure, appearing in play after play to delight the audience with familiar jokes and keep the complex mechanics of the plot turning.

Hetairai, the fashionable courtesans of Athens, made their first appearance as characters only after Aristophanes who made do with mute dancing-girls as the only female alternative to the "drag" persona. Social mores were in a state of flux. Eubulus, one of the earlier writers of fourth-century comedy, used women's names as titles for several of his plays. One of his works, *The Garland-Sellers* (*Stephanopolides*), had a plot that curiously anticipated Colette's *Gigi* of many centuries later. It told of a *hetaira* unwilling to have her daughter jeopardize her professional career by falling in love. There was also a chorus listing prominent *hetairai* of the time by name.

All this was a far cry from Aristophanes, though some traces of mythological burlesque did hang on. Our chief evidence for "the Gods at play" is a Roman New Comedy imitation, Plautus' *Amphitruo*, composed perhaps in about 190 B.C., but based on a fourth-century original. This is a particularly interesting work for it has clear affinities with both Greek tragedy and comedy. As we will soon see, fifth-century tragedy may well have proved a stronger influence than Old Comedy on the plays of Menander.

The subject of *Amphitruo* is the birth of one of the most pervasive and popular figures of folklore, the demigod Herakles (Latin Hercules). In tragedy, this theme had attracted Euripides and, perhaps, Sophocles. In comedy, there was a direct source in *The Long Night* by Plato.[2] Euripides' tragedy may well have been a model of moral complexity. Plautus contents himself with the risible convolutions of infidelity.

Jupiter (Zeus), king and father of the gods, casts lustful eyes on Alcumena (Greek, Alkmene), the wife of the general Amphitruo. To make his conquest easier he disguises himself as her husband. A subordinate deity, the mischievous Mercury (Hermes) takes on the likeness of Amphitruo's slave Sosia. These identical impersonations produce a string of predictable complications. Plautus' play, however, is prevented from becoming a mere sex-farce by the enormous dignity and sympathy accorded to the deluded Alcumena. This element, not one for which Plautus is elsewhere noted, may well go back to the greater delicacy of Plautus' source.

Amphitruo's distress at his wife's apparent infidelity is assuaged when the god reveals his identity:

> Be of good heart, Amphitruo; I stand by you and yours.
> No need to be afraid. The prophets and the soothsayers,
> Send them away; I'll tell what's past and yet to come.
> Better than all of these; for I am Jupiter. (Plautus
> *Amphitruo*, 1132–6, trans. P. Arnott)

Thus the divine parentage of Hercules is assured, and Amphitruo caps the play with an appeal to the audience for a round of applause "for the sake of Jupiter in the highest" (1146).[3]

However original Plautus' contribution may be, comedy has clearly taken a new direction with the passing of Aristophanes. The transition can hardly have been as abrupt as this would seem to suggest. Some satire was still at the expense of contemporary personalities, though these were apparently not politicians. We may add philosophers to the parasites and *hetairai* mentioned above. A certain amount of toothless political reference was still made, although this was dwindling rapidly: by Menander's time it had disappeared.

THE INFLUENCE OF TRAGEDY

That a Plautine comedy should have partly tragic antecedents is not surprising, for by the Hellenistic period the worlds of tragedy and comedy had begun to deal with similar issues. In the fifth century the genres had been distinct at least until Euripides. No tragic playwright, as far as we know, entered the comic festivals, nor did Aristophanes ever try his hand at tragedy. A meeting-ground did exist in the satyr play, the short, comic afterpiece to complete a tragic trio. The chorus of satyrs, the buffoons of Greek mythology, were acolytes of Dionysus, the theatre's patron god.

The plots, from the examples that we know, were popular mythological burlesques. Satyr plays seem to have had a number of functions. They served to give the audience necessary light relief. More seriously, and in a more complex manner, the satyrs gave an affirmation of the power of survival and renewal in a world laid waste by contrary forces. Perhaps for this reason alone, the satyr play is known to have maintained its stage popularity, not only alongside the performances of Menander and his contemporaries at various Greek festivals, but also way beyond New Comedy adaptations in Rome and into the Christian era.[4]

The burlesque factor of the satyr play as it was associated with classical tragedy did not mean that there could be no lighter note in the tragedies themselves. Even Aeschylus has his lighter moments, and both Aeschylus and Sophocles occasionally introduce characters whose earthy humanity contrasts with the doom-laden situations into which they have intruded. But, for a good part of the fifth century, Tragedy and Old Comedy went their separate ways. Tragedy was abstract, austere, dignified: comedy pulsed with the rawness of everyday experience. As the fifth century moved on, however, and as Athens prepared to enter the devastating Peloponnesian War these extremes began to overlap.

Aeschylus died in 456 B.C. Later fifth-century tragedy was dominated by Sophocles and Euripides. Near contemporaries, they lived through the same experiences and competed against each other in the same festivals for the better part of fifty years. In method and intention, however, Sophocles and Euripides are poles apart. While both draw their stories from the traditional body of subject matter—mythology, folklore, the rich legends of individual cities—Sophocles tackles major issues in a form that echoes the world of the Homeric hero but diverts the themes into valid messages for a new generation.

By comparison, Euripides is the playwright of discomfiture. He stands apart from his sources, questions them, and, as often as not, diminishes them. His stance is, from the beginning, critical. Are these characters plausible, he asks, in terms of recognizable human behavior? If real men and women found themselves in the extraordinary circumstances of received myth, how would they conduct themselves? Euripides' self-appointed task is to humanize myth and legend, to divest his protagonists of their heroic qualities and superhuman pretensions, and to examine the more dubious values that their glamour conceals. In such an approach humor—albeit mordant, sometimes cruel humor—has a proper part to play.

Euripides' refusal to confine himself within existing patterns leads him to cross genres and create plays that do not lend themselves to easy classification. Significantly, his earliest surviving play is not a tragedy at all. More romance with the potential for tragedy, it has attracted the description of "protosatyric" because it was presented in the festival slot customarily reserved for a satyr play. *Alkestis* was the last item of a controversial bill presented in 438 B.C. To be fair, it does retain some features of the traditional satyr play. There is a strong element of boisterous farce when Herakles gets drunk. But the prevailing tone is of social comedy, questioning contemporary Greek attitudes in a manner potentially offensive to some sections of a male-dominated Athenian audience. It is here, more than anywhere in Aristophanes, that the seeds of Menandrian comedy are truly to be found.

The plot of *Alkestis* revolves around Admetus, king of Pherae, who has been reprieved from death by his protective god, Apollo, on condition that he provides a substitute. After he has canvassed his friends and relatives in vain, his wife Alkestis offers to go in his place. We have, therefore, a story which, played straight, would celebrate one of the most enduring of Greek prejudices, the subjugation of the female to the male. As one of the characters proposes, all women should behave this way: otherwise, there is no point in marriage.

Euripides, typically, refuses to play it straight. Instead, he offers us a domestic problem-drama in which what now appear to be the arrogance and chauvinism of the husband are under serious debate. In the light of Alkestis' devotion, Admetus is revealed as whining and self-centered, so blinded by his frantic attempts to prolong his days that, even at the moment of his wife's death, he can only complain that no one will be left to look after him and his children.

Though clearly attitudes toward kingship as well as toward marriage have undergone enormous changes, it is difficult to see Admetus as other than isolated in a world that is hard put to sympathize. He is finally redeemed from misery by the glimmerings of conscience and that very quality of charity that first won him Apollo's approval. Life in itself, he realizes, is not enough. Without a partner, shorn of ties and companionship, he has been reduced to a husk of his former self. His change of heart is rewarded by the miraculous intervention of his old friend Herakles, whom he has welcomed into his house without revealing that Alkestis has just died. When Herakles discovers what has happened, he goes to wrestle with Death and succeeds in restoring Alkestis to her chastened spouse.

Alkestis clearly is not a tragedy, though some critics have been prone to describe it as such. Still less is it a satyr play despite its comic sequence: a fairy-tale, rather, with a happy ending which begins by stating the inevitability of death and ends with a joyful resurrection. Although the events that provoke the action are from traditional myth, the play bears many of the character traits of a Menander piece. Admetus is portrayed as no legendary figure from the remote past but an all too fallible Athenian, ruling as paterfamilias of a large estate. Herakles proves the divine savior, but he is initially an ill-mannered house-guest who drinks too much at dinner. Admetus and his father, squabbling across Alkestis' corpse, are working out some atavistic struggle between the generations, but they are also human beings, angry, jealous, and more than a little ridiculous as they grapple to score points and assuage their consciences.

As any comedy of Menander a hundred and twenty years later, this play of Euripides is packed with domestic detail that could have come from any number of houses in Euripides' Athens. The funeral arrangements, with scattered leaves and urns for the mourners to wash themselves at the door; the muffled voices, the shaven heads; the children crying, bereaved brother comforting little sister; the resentful servants, the house left dusty and untidy by the mistress's death. Apart from the leading characters the *dramatis personae* are humble people, domestics, subordinates, and familiars of the house, including a chorus of neighbors come to pay their respects, almost comically unsure about whether or not they should yet be wearing mourning. We are introduced to an old servant weeping at the loss of her mistress, to another, complaining of the extra work brought on by having to manage both a funeral and the master's demanding guest. Even the gods, Apollo and a personified Death, squabble in the Prologue like advocates over the protocol of dying.

Compare this, then, with the story of Knemon in Menander's *Duskolos, The Malcontent*. Knemon is a man who has chosen to isolate himself from the world. His wife and stepson have moved out, leaving him with a daughter and a single servant. He complains about neighbors and strangers alike. Apparently, he is the exact antithesis of Admetus, the "perfect host." But when he finds himself in trouble, Gorgias, the stepson, helps him out and, after considerable heart-searching, Knemon comes to realize that no man is an island. Again the play is a mine of domestic detail and routine. Here, however, there is a love interest with a young man who has fallen for Knemon's daughter and the intrigue revolves around various attempts to fix up a match.

The status of the characters is different; the situation in Menander is localized to the Attica countryside, and the death in Admetus' family is an event of major consequence. In tone, however, the similarities are marked. The god Pan introduces *The Malcontent* to assure the audience of his interest in securing a happy end: Apollo does much the same in *Alkestis*, disarming the threat from Death. Both plays feature believable families. In both plays it is the intervention of servants which serves as the dramatic turning point. Most importantly, both plays hinge on the capacity of flawed leading characters to learn from experience: not to suffer instant conversion— Euripides and Menander are both too canny for that—but to come to appreciate their selfishness in a manner that offers a moral lesson couched in palatable terms.

Alkestis is a milestone in the history of the Greek drama. It appears to be wholly original. Within its short length it breached a number of sacred traditions and probably made a portion of its first audience thoroughly uneasy. The mood to which it gave license spills over into more obviously tragic works. Euripides' earliest extant tragedy, *Medea*, was written seven years later. Like *Alkestis*, it is set in the legendary past. As in *Alkestis*, Euripides sets out to humanize and familiarize the personages of the drama, infusing them with contemporary vividness and urgency. Although in the last analysis *Medea* may be read as a study of decayed values and retributive justice in an amoral world, its immediate impact is familial and domestic. It is about unfaithfulness, divorce, and a house in turmoil.

This was seldom Sophocles' way, although the descriptions of Deianira's domestic routine in *Women of Trachis* (?c.445 B.C.) indicate that he was capable of innovative method. Deianira shows all the frustrations and loneliness of being married to a legend. *Women of Trachis* is exceptional in Sophocles' work, but Euripides is regularly concerned to show us ordinary human beings, suffering a recognizable dilemma in a familiar environment. From the opening of *Medea* we are plunged into the atmosphere of family crisis. The first scene concentrates on servants' gossip: husband and wife are at loggerheads, the children are in danger. We see the children, pathetic innocents running home from play, ignorant of the danger that surrounds them. Even the minor characters are brought to us in memorable detail. The children's old tutor relays to their nurse a rumor picked up in town:

> I was passing the place where the old men sit
> Playing at draughts, near the Pirean spring.
> Pretending not to listen, I overheard one say
> That Creon . . . (*Medea* 67–70, trans. Jeremy Brooks, from *Euripides Plays: One*: Methuen, 1988.)

This is a sharp vignette of everyday life as it was plainly lived in and about a hundred Greek villages and is later seen to be lived with few alterations in the world of Menander. We can picture vividly one of the most familiar meeting places of any Greek community, the public water supply. We see the village elders passing their day as they still do in every Greek village; we see the tutor, inquisitive, sly, ducking into a corner as he realizes he may acquire some profitable information if he stays out of sight. Later, when the chorus assembles, they make no formal, marching entry. Rather they seem to drift in, all wagging tongues, greedy to find out what new misfortune has afflicted their neighbor: women out of Kazantzakis rather than out of Homer.

Euripides' fondness for the mundane and domestic, for divesting tragedy of its aloof grandeur, was regarded with suspicion in his own time. Many clearly thought of it as degrading the nature of tragedy. Aristophanes, who we can usually assume is recording the popular opinion, makes it a principal point of attack in *Frogs*. His spokesman in the comedy is Aeschylus, the senior playwright, the Grand Old Man of Greek theatre.

Aeschylus is made to disapprove of Euripides' propensity for lowborn characters. He parodies the commonplace subject matter of a typical Euripidean lyric:

Ah me, me miserable!
I sat there spinning,
Spi-i-i-i-i-inning,
Busy fingers flicking the flax,
Making little balls, balls
To creep out of the house in the dawnlight
And sell in that stall in the market.
And now he's gone, gone,
On fluttery, feathery winglets
My cock has flown.
Oh woe! Oh no! (*Frogs* 1346–54, trans. Kenneth McLeish, from *Aristophanes Plays: Two*, Methuen, 1993.)

The suggestion that for Euripides the loss of a rooster seems as tragic as the downfall of an Ikaros or a Bellerophon is, of course, comic license. Aristophanes comes closer to real dramatic criticism when he has Aeschylus comment on Euripides' prosy dramatic language:

AESCHYLUS: We've a duty to show what's right and proper.

EURIPIDES: So to show what's right and proper
    Everyone must speak in high-flown language,
    Must they, all these characters of yours,
    Instead of like human beings?

AESCHYLUS: Dignified sentiments require dignified language,
    You great numbskull.
    Heroes and gods should never talk like commoners:
    Nor dress like them either. (1056–61, translation Walton)

But that is what Euripides' characters do: they do talk like commoners, not heroes: and they do dress to suit their station. Euripides' realism did not confine itself to language and situation. His stage settings, though still utilizing the traditional fabric of the open-air theatre, attempted a greater degree of scenic identification: no longer a blank, ubiquitous acting space, but giving an impression of actual buildings in a real-life location. This aspect of his work, and its consequences for Menander, are discussed in greater length in Chapter 3. Aeschylus' criticisms are barely exaggeration, more a reflection of the changes that the end of the century has heralded in theatrical technique.

These changes in the externals of tragedy—setting, situation, language—inevitably worked a modification in the nature of tragedy itself. In bringing tragedy down to earth, making it the story of ordinary men and women, Euripides is pointing out that few of us, in our everyday lives, are remotely tragic. The commonplace intervenes. Banality treads on the heels of dignity. As Euripides' career extends, therefore, he creates what is virtually a new kind of play in which tragic grandeur is lightened by everyday observation. Rather than tragedy, we might perhaps talk more appropriately of tragicomedy or, as earlier, romance. The more one considers such material, the more clear it becomes that, whatever innovations are justly attributed to Menander's specific vision, no claims can be made for him as the inventor of stage realism. He may have perfected a tendency to which the drama of the fourth century B.C. was advancing. He may also have led the way in placing living characters onto the Greek stage. He was not the first to portray human predicaments that could touch the sensibilities of his audience through an immediate empathy rather than through some exalted and lofty vision.

Among the later plays of Euripides (later but still, it must be remembered, written seventy years before Menander was born), two are particularly valuable pointers toward Menander's New Comedy. The first is *Helen*, produced in 412 B.C. Here Euripides adopts a revisionist version of the famous legend about the Trojan War. In this account Helen was never kidnapped by Paris and never went to Troy. Only her wraith made the journey, an apparition fashioned by Hera in response to failing to win the gold medal in the beauty competition against her fellow Olympians. The real Helen has been spirited away to Egypt. When the play opens, she is discovered plaintively lamenting the problems of having been born from an egg and wondering how much longer she can keep the local Pharaoh at bay. Menelaus, her husband, appears. The war is over and, like so many of the Greek heroes, he has been shipwrecked while homeward bound.

There ensues a half-sentimental, half-comic recognition scene, as Menelaus, dressed only in a scrap of sailcloth, confronts the spitting image of the wife for whom he has just fought a ten-year war and who, when he last saw her, was back on the beach with his shipwrecked crew. "My problem is, I already have a wife," he announces lamely. Helen, who has spent the last ten years fending off the lascivious attentions of the importunate Pharaoh, faces the prospect of losing her husband to the wraith. Better the Helen you know. . . . Then a diffident messenger arrives from the shore to tell Menelaus that his wife—nobody has told him anything about wraiths—for whom they have all been fighting a war for the last ten years, has just evaporated before their eyes. All too aware of how implausible his story sounds, he displays an almost tangible relief on catching sight of the real Helen: "Oh, you've been here all the time, have you? And me going on about you flying through the heavens and that sort of thing."

Properly reunited, Helen and Menelaus plot how they may escape from the Pharaoh's clutches and how to get Menelaus the bath he sorely needs. A plan that depends on the false news of Menelaus' death recalls Orestes' revenge against Helen's sister Klytemnestra and her lover Aegisthus, as recounted by Aeschylus and Sophocles. Success here is never in doubt. The Pharaoh is deluded into providing an escape ship, supposedly to be used in a memorial ceremony. Menelaus and Helen sail off into the sunset and live happily ever after.

The same plot device was to serve centuries later for more than one composer of comic opera. Although the play masquerades as tragedy by virtue of its presentation position at the Great Dionysia, it has little in common with Sophocles' *Ajax* or Euripides' *Andromache* (both dates unknown) and *Iphigeneia in Aulis* (produced posthumously), three other tragedies in which Menelaus is a major character.

Although the sense of the futility of war pervades the play, the theme is treated in almost absurdist terms. It is no more serious than is the consideration of the inevitability of death in *Alkestis*, a play that most obviously shares *Helen*'s tone. Nor, as we shall see, is it that much different from the opening of Menander's *The Shield*, where the grief at the loss of a loved one is fully expressed, deflected only by the audience's privileged knowledge.

The other play of Euripides which appears influential for the rise of New Comedy is *Ion* whose date is uncertain but which was probably written and first performed in the later years of the Peloponnesian War, just prior to the time Euripides left Athens to go and live in Macedon.

Ion is the story of an abandoned child whose parentage is in question. He has been brought up as a temple servant at Apollo's shrine at Delphi. To the shrine come Xuthus and Kreusa, a long married but childless couple, seeking to learn from the oracle how their union may be blessed with issue. At one time or another both parents come to believe that Ion is their illegitimate son.

The play builds up a baffling complex of pretense and subterfuge. Nothing is ever quite what it seems. The chorus are pilgrims to the Delphic shrine whose first entry consists of a paean of praise to the quality of the decoration on the temple front. "We've got something like that in Athens," one member remarks, cheekily pointing to the dual stage illusion of location and setting.

The god Hermes has introduced the play in a Prologue where he asserts that Ion is really Kreusa's son, born as a result of her rape by Apollo and exposed by her in the cave where the rape took place. This is often the position in which the heroine of New Comedy will find herself. A further link is provided by the provision of a set of convenient recognition tokens by which, when the time arrives, all will be revealed. The plot is compounded by Apollo's apparent attempt to cover up his part in any of this. He tells the gullible Xuthus, a character almost as dim-witted as Menelaus in *Helen*, that the first person he meets after emerging from the oracle will be his son Xuthus, who presumably appreciating that he, too, could have once become a father unknowingly, rushes out and espies Ion. His hurried embrace is wrongly interpreted by Ion who is uncomfortable at being physically accosted in public by a total stranger.

Things are now becoming more and more complicated as even the Chorus begin to smell a rat. Kreusa upsets everything further by trying to poison Ion. Eventually, a resolution is forthcoming when the Priestess of the temple arrives with the cradle in which Ion was abandoned. The only trouble with that is that the cradle looks remarkably new, as Ion is quick to point out, and again the suspicion arises that the whole thing is a put-up job. Ion is prepared to accept Kreusa as his mother but cannot believe that Apollo is his father. He is only prevented from running into the shrine to confront the god directly by the arrival, *ex machina*, not of Apollo, or even Hermes, but of Athene, who makes a lame excuse about why Apollo could not come himself, Athene persuades Ion and Kreusa to accept what they have been told and return to Athens with Xuthus who hasn't been told the half of it.

Ion is a play of constant surprises. The blatantly comic side is predicated on an acknowledgment of the stage as a stage. Much of Aristophanes' technique is similarly self-aware, but the range of dramatic devices and in-jokes in *Ion* has few parallels in tragedy. *Helen* is high comedy, an Offenbachian romp through familiar legend. *Ion* combines comedy with a serious study of a boy growing up and faced with the question of his own antecedents. T. S. Eliot used it as his model for *The Confidential Clerk*. More significantly, *Ion* heralds the kind of play that can come to the final curtain without all the problems being resolved. There are still questions to be asked at the end and, whether or not Euripides intended it, there lingers in the mind the possibility that perhaps we too have not heard the whole story: that we too are victims of a masquerade.

It is in this, linked to the question mark raised first in *Alkestis* about how the characters may fare after the play is over, that New Comedy is most obviously invoked. Menander will go on to write plays in which the issues are the same: marital complications, split families, disputed children. The means of resolution will be similar too. In *Ion*, the cardinal factor is a stage prop, the cradle in which the baby was abandoned. *The Arbitration (Epitrepontes)* of Menander revolves around a similar use of recognition tokens left with an exposed child. More than this, Menander will pick up on

Euripides' capacity for human concern. His characters will be "serious," because, however foolish or misguided, we come to be bothered about them. If the story was ours, they could be us.

Euripides' works were not merely available to Menander in reading form. They were still alive in the repertoire, the most popular being the romance plays discussed above. It is hardly fanciful to suggest that Menander would have seen productions of *Alkestis*, of *Ion*, *Iphigeneia in Tauris*, and *Helen*. Although the object of intense interest among his contemporaries, Euripides remained a controversial figure. He lived to confound expectation. He resembled George Bernard Shaw[5]—too prickly, too honest, and too downright clever to make his contemporaries warm to him.[6] The festival audiences responded in kind. In all his career Euripides won only four victories and ended his life voluntarily, or otherwise, in exile.

His posthumous reputation, however, was enormous. The rest of the world had caught up with him. Things he had said with deliberate intent to shock were now new orthodoxies. In an age when traditional religious beliefs were waning, Euripides' casual blasphemy was common currency. Just as importantly, a theatre newly turned professional realized that Euripides had created a gallery of star roles with more than local appeal.

When Lykurgus, late in the fourth century, prepared an official edition of the fifth-century tragedies, he drew, in part, from the memories of living actors who carried the roles in their heads. The Athenian collection, transported to Alexandria, became the source for the manuscripts that provide our own texts. We have no more than the seven plays by Aeschylus and seven by Sophocles. Nineteen Euripides plays survive: and this difference is almost certainly due to the greater popularity among performers. Would that Menander's oeuvres had survived in similar fashion.

Aeschylus, who depended so heavily on his chorus, had largely vanished from the repertoire: a classic but a shelf classic. Some plays of Sophocles were still performed up to Menander's time, but Euripides was preeminent. Ancient commentators were well aware that characteristic dramatic devices developed by the tragic writers were subsumed into the comedies. Satyrus, Euripides' biographer, noted[7] that the familiar elements of the plays of Menander and his contemporaries—discussion, rapes, suppositious children, recognition—had all been brought to perfection by Euripides. The plays of the fifth-century masters are not classics simply because they are the only plays to have survived. The actual plays that we have may be the result of luck to a great extent, but there is no doubt that the Athenians of the fourth century knew who their greatest playwrights had been. When Lykurgus rebuilt the theatre of Dionysus, he erected statues of the tragic triad, Aeschylus, Sophocles, and Euripides. We may take this, together with Lykurgus' compilation of an official edition of the texts, as the adoption of the fifth-century tragedies as "classics," authoritative, venerable, if in danger of becoming remote.

For Menander they have become a source of allusion and proverb. Lines from tragedy are cited with almost biblical resonance. In *The Arbitration* Syros examines the birth tokens of the disputed child and comments, "You've seen tragedies on stage, I'm sure of it. You know what it's all about" (*The Arbitration* 325–26). Various examples are quoted of the appearance of recognition tokens in tragedy, and Onesimos later delivers a quotation from Euripides' *Auge*. In *The Woman from Samos* Demeas introduces the story of Danae: "You know that old play, don't you, where Zeus is transformed into a shower of gold?" (*The Woman from Samos*, 589–90).

The stage of New Comedy may well have offered visual reminders of tragedy too. In *The Shield* it is likely that the *ekkuklema*, the stage truck, was used, in the older tragic manner, to roll out from the *skene* and reveal a body: the same may have happened for the injured Knemon in Act Five of *The Malcontent*. Arnott noted that in the same play the lonely figure of the ingenue, emerging from her father's jail-like cottage to fetch water, may be a deliberate attempt to recall Euripides' Elektra in similar position.

LOST COMEDY

Some mention, however brief, must be made at this point of the multitude of writers of comedy in the fourth century who have disappeared almost without trace into the sands of time or, perhaps, Egypt. Forty or more writers of comedy are known by name from the period between Aristophanes and Menander, and we have the titles of almost six hundred plays. Yet apart from the two late Aristophanes already discussed, *Women in Power* and *Wealth*, no text survives nor anything that as much as resembles a whole scene. Hence there is the inevitable silence over a good sixty years about what was still a living and changing tradition.

Many playwrights of the period were non-Athenian, which in itself suggests the onset of cosmopolitanism. Among the best known of Menander's contemporaries, Diphilus was from Sinope on the Black Sea and Philemon originally from Syracuse. Both were sufficiently popular to feed the Roman comedies, the *fabulae Palliatae* of the second century B.C. Diphilus provided the original for Plautus' *Casina* and *Rudens*, and Philemon for his *Mercator*, *Mostellaria*, and *Trinummus*. Apollodorus who furnished the originals for two of Terence's six plays was a Sicilian.

Sadly, quotations and fragments are a poor substitute for whole plays, and that is all that remains of any of these playwrights. Heroic, if occasionally unconvincing, efforts by T.B.L. Webster ensured that any evidence there was should be most thoroughly examined. Certainly, fragments, however small, when the attribution is sound, offer evidence for character types, and dramatic situations including love affairs, rapes, and recognitions.[8] Webster also provided provisional datings for individual plays, from festival records or internal reference.

All in all, however, it is a somewhat dispiriting process. What does emerge positively is a multitude of possible echoes linking past and future and suggesting that the playwrights were creating their work for an audience versed in a living theatrical tradition. It may not have been every individual in the fifteen thousand-strong house who could recognize the quotations, visual and aural, with which the productions were peppered. Nonetheless, we are now in a position to place Menander in his full historic context and to consider from that standpoint such complete work of his as does survive. Such an evaluation can safely be based on two major assumptions. The first is that the playwright himself was familiar with the history of his own theatre and its substantial literature. The second is that the sophistication of the Greek audience had advanced sufficiently far in the two hundred or so years since Thespis for a reasonable proportion of them to find in the plays of Menander all the subtleties that subsequent eras were to attribute to him.

NOTES

1. Oliver Taplin, *Comic Angels*, Oxford: Oxford University Press, 1993.

2. Not, of course, Plato the philosopher, but a well-known playwright of the same name who was still working in the first decade of the fourth century.

3. A similar incident involving Zeus in disguise is cited by Demeas in Act IV of Menander's *The Woman from Samos* when trying to convince Nikeratos of his daughter's respectability.

4. Only one example of a satyr play has survived complete, Euripides' *Cyclops*, based on a familiar episode from Homer's *Odyssey* (see *Euripides Plays: Two*, London: Methuen, 1991).

5. This is a comparison made in a celebrated essay by Gilbert Norwood in *Euripides and Shaw*, London: Methuen, 1921.

6. But see Erich Segal (ed.), *Euripides, a Collection of Critical Essays*, Prentice-Hall, NJ, 1963, p. 11, for an alternative view.

7. Satyrus, *Vita Euripidis*, of Oxyrhynchus Papyri, 1176, London, Egypt Exploration Society, 1912.

8. See T.B.L. Webster, *Studies in Later Greek Comedy*, Manchester: Manchester University Press, 1953, which includes chapters on both Diphilus and Apollodorus and their influence on Roman New Comedy: see also his *Studies in Menander*, 2nd ed., Manchester: Manchester University Press, 1960, pp. 162–75.

Chapter 2

Menander in Time and Place

Menander was born some forty years after the death of Aristophanes and did not begin writing for the stage until the last twenty years of the fourth century B.C. The second half of the fourth century was a time of change in more things than the theatre. Audiences had already learned to accept a social emphasis in the plays that they saw, tragedies included, but this was symptomatic of a whole new climate of political and economic pressures that had rapidly reshaped the Mediterranean world.

In earlier times Greece had evolved slowly and painfully as a country of numerous independent city-states. Each had its own constitution, its particular presiding deities, and its own racial affiliations. Each had its own dialect, marked not merely by differences of accent but by idiosyncratic grammar and vocabulary, in extreme cases virtually distinct languages. Each city jealously guarded its own independence and watched aggressively for supposed slights from others. Greeks as a whole recognized that certain qualifications set them apart from the barbarian nations, the non-Greeks; but aside from this, little recognition of a national identity existed.[1] Greek history before the early fifth century B.C., therefore, was written piecemeal and distinguished by intercity violence, with first one community and then another coming temporarily to the fore.

In the early decades of the fifth century, this model began to change as the Greek cities were forced into a semblance of unity by fear of the common foe, Persia, for the first and last time until the threatened invasion from

Macedon late in the fourth century. The eventual defeat of Persia allowed the Athenians to establish hegemony, almost by default, over many of the Greek city-states and the islands, under the pretext of providing a necessary buffer against future reprisals. The Persians might return. They never in fact, did, but the threat remained and Athens made the most of it, pouring large amounts of protection money into the rebuilding of the city. This was the period that saw a massive building program transform Athens into the wonder of its own and every other age. It saw the final formation of the Athenian democracy. In the theatre it produced the great tragedians, Aeschylus, Sophocles, and Euripides and, latterly, the comic inspiration of Aristophanes.

Aristophanes' comedies sum up their time. They abound with energy and invention. They are obsessed, though not uncritically, with Athens as the center of the universe. They burst with a self-confidence that allows their author to mock his city's most hallowed institutions. As in the British or the Hungarian empires at their height, they give the impression that the existing order is forever and that any impertinence is licensed, for nothing can go seriously astray.

It was not, of course, forever. The wheels were already becoming loose while Aristophanes was still a schoolboy. Athenian empire-building fell victim to a combination of fatal weaknesses in the Athenian temperament and the jealousy of other strong cities that Athens had thrown into the shade. All of Aristophanes' plays except the very last were performed against the background of a war against Sparta whose traditional military supremacy had been jeopardized by the naval strength of Athens. The Peloponnesian War eventually broke out in 431 B.C., lasted for most of the rest of the century, and concluded with a decisive Spartan victory.

Athens entered the war arrogant in power and wealth, and left it whimpering. The long walls giving access to a lifeline of the sea were destroyed. The empire was shattered, her financial resources exhausted. The conclusion of hostilities, however, marked more than the shifting of Athens from prime place. It presaged a change in the traditional pattern of life for many cities besides.

Out of the detritus of war grew a tangle of changed attitudes and shifting alliances. Athens, once so proud of democracy, fell prey to committees whose anonymous and unlovely names are the very coinage of despotism: the Thirty, the Eleven, the Ten. Spartan overlordship was succeeded by a quisling government, which, in turn, was succeeded by a series of shifts and compromises that halfheartedly claimed to resurrect the democratic spirit. Democracy itself was suspect; had not democracy, after all, lost the war?

No less sweeping changes were observed in the victors' camp. Sparta, having spent three decades in the aggressive denunciation of imperialism, drifted into the novel and alien posture of heir to the Athenian Empire, and embarked on imperialistic ventures of its own. Athens formed an alliance with Thebes, one of the bitterest of former enemies, and Sparta warred on its old ally, Corinth.

Such shifts of loyalty were not, of course, in themselves new. They had always formed part of the traditional Greek way of life. What was new was a growing tendency to look beyond the traditional boundaries. The fourth century ushered in a more cosmopolitan spirit. In the past, it had been an article of faith that the individual's ultimate loyalty was to his own community. He was bound to it by indissoluble ties, and he could realize his full potential only through the city that had nurtured him. In the aftermath of the Peloponnesian War, the old certainties could no longer be so easily affirmed. Many, out of self-protection, sought larger allegiances that took them beyond the city walls and into strange company. Armies of mercenaries, the flotsam of thirty years of campaigning, offered themselves to the highest bidder. A Greek army campaigned for a pretender to the Persian throne, fighting a string of battles in which Greek loyalties had no conceivable part. An Athenian admiral commanded a Persian fleet against Sparta.

Concerned for their security in a world that had become more dangerous, the city-states began to look wider and abandon ancient prejudices. In various parts of Greece, individual cities abandoned their traditional autonomy to enter a protective federation. In Athens Isokrates, rhetorician and political philosopher, found it opportune to preach the virtues of panhellenism. Hellenism, he argued, was a state of mind, not an accident of birth. Character and intellect, not race alone, should determine who was Greek and who was not. Moschion's reaction in *The Woman from Samos*, written late in the fourth century, to his father's concern about bringing an illegitimate child into the world is no liberal novelty when he claims: "I'm perfectly serious. I swear it. I can see no difference between being of one race or of another. To anyone who believes in justice, if a man's good, he's legitimate, if he's bad, he's a bastard" (*The Woman from Samos* 140–42).

Such changes in attitude were inevitably gradual and attended by times of concerted political confusion. Much of the history of the years after the conclusion of the mighty Peloponnesian War reads as a depressing catalogue of minor cities slicing chunks out of one another. In the first half of the fourth century, Thebes, the legendary birthplace of Oedipus and Antigone, with its aristocratic constitution and handpicked military elite, graduated to being the dominant city of Greece. Sparta had become the enemy to be watched. When the Thebans inflicted a major defeat on the Spartans at the battle of Leuktra in 371 B.C., the effects proved far-reaching. Spartan power was curbed and with it the one land army that might have proved capable of providing effective resistance to the new threat that was so soon to emerge from Macedon.

Theban reaction to becoming the most powerful of the Greek states was to create new communities overriding earlier local boundaries. These were to serve as magnet cities, which would attract large populations and provide a buffer against Spartan aggression. One such example of urban planning may still be seen in ruinous disarray and overshadowed by an ugly modern namesake. Its founders called it Megalopolis, a name without imagination or local roots. It means simply "Big City," thereby revealing that the age of the bureaucrat had already arrived. It contained, among other engineered delights, the largest theatre in mainland Greece, designed to suck in pleasure-seekers from a wide surrounding area. This, apparently, it completely failed to do. We would do well to note this severance of long tradition. In the fifth century the theatre had been an organic part of the community, located in its sacred heart and serving a multiplicity of artistic, civic, and religious functions. The purpose-built theatre of Megalopolis, so lavishly designed and so quickly redundant, foreshadows a new theatrical world, a world of professional players and high finance.

Theban federalism, to be fair, did provide an alternative form of unity to any offered by the imperialism of Athens or Sparta, but it was to prove unequal to coping with the new force emerging from the north. This was the kingdom of Macedon. The people of central and southern Greece were inclined, and still are, to regard Macedon as a primitive, though wholly Greek, outpost in the wilderness, much as the English have always treated Scotland as a marginal part of Britain or as the Americans have considered the Yukon. Macedon was peopled, men believed, by a race who were at best semibarbarian. This rugged domain, however, had its own riches and traditions. In the closing years of the war with Sparta, the tragedian Euripides had found a friendly exile there, when Athens had become too uncomfortable to hold him. Macedon was now catapulted into national attention as a new contender in Greek power politics. Further south, Greeks still squabbled with Greeks. In 356 the Phokians attacked Apollo's prophetic shrine at Delphi and plundered its riches to pay mercenaries. Further north the baby was born who would become known as Alexander the Great.

The moving spirit behind the rise of Macedon was the man later known as Philip II. His entree to power was his guardianship of a young nephew, prospective heir to the Macedonian kingdom. Philip first brought internal security to Macedon by subjugating his dissident neighbors and then assumed the royal title in his own right. Within a few years he had created a strong and united Macedon, a new capital at Pella, and a military presence to be reckoned with.

His new eminence brought him invitations to act as power broker, intervening in Greek disputes elsewhere. Other cities thought of him variously as a blessing and a curse. Opinion was particularly divided in Athens, where one faction regarded him as a potential savior and the hope of the future, while others created a powerful lobby against him. His most prominent and certainly his noisiest opponent was the orator Demosthenes who issued a sequence of vitriolic speeches attacking not only Philip and all his works but all his local Athenian supporters. A Theban/Athenian alliance was forged but suffered a defeat at the battle of Chaironeia in 338 B.C. which was to color the political complexion of Athens throughout the life of Menander who was no more than four years old at the time.

Philip was now in a position to impose political settlement on the whole of Greece. In 338 and 337 the leading Greek cities convened at Corinth, paying Philip the supreme tribute, as well as acknowledging the realities of their situation, by electing him as *strategos*, their leader of combined military operations. Attica was never invaded, and Athens retained control of several of the islands, but it became clear to all but the most rabid traditionalist that Athens was no longer a political force of any real note.

It is clear that Philip entertained plans to reverse the course of Mediterranean history. In the fifth century, Greece had been invaded by Persia. In the fourth century, Persia was to be invaded by Greeks. The only question was whether the Greeks would react with a semblance of unity long enough to make an invasion effective. Philip, if anyone, was the man to provide inspiration and a sense of purpose.

The project was halted by Philip's untimely death. Struck down by an assassin in 336 B.C., he bequeathed his throne to his son Alexander. The boy lost no time. Elected *strategos* in his father's place, Alexander first pacified local resistance in the north and then swept through Greece on a punitive mission against Thebes. With domestic affairs settled, he embarked on a triumphant tour of foreign conquest that earned him the title of "The Great" and elevated him, in many people's eyes, to the status of at least semidivinity.

Alexander's character has no place in this book. His achievments do, for they created a new and vastly larger Greek world, a world with a different geography, with changed imperatives and a new vision of humanity. The age that Alexander inaugurated, the age that we have come to call "Hellenistic," was the time of Menander's formative years: the changing world picture created a new domestic frame for his plays.

Antipater, one of Alexander's generals, was left behind with half the army to govern Macedonia and to keep a watchful eye on Greece while the young king embarked on a tour of conquest that took him all the way to India. One of the problems that continually plagued Alexander was the readiness of his opponents to foment rebellion back home. Thousands of miles and a wide sea away, he found it easier to make conquests than to keep control of them. With the rest of the troops, Alexander cut into Persia and beyond and won a series of decisive battles: the Granikus, Tyre, Gargemela, and the Hydaspes. Ancient empires toppled into his possession. Persia, the old enemy, now hardly a threat, became a Greek dependency. Egypt, where Alexander visited the shrine of Zeus in the desert and had himself proclaimed the son of god, succumbed with hardly a protest. Alexander was halted at last, not by the resistance of his enemies, but by the recalcitrance of his own soldiers. Isolated and afraid, far from their familiar seas and trapped in a march that seemed likely to go on forever, they demanded to return. Forced to comply, Alexander turned his face toward Greece again. But the luck that had attended his outward voyage now deserted him. On his way home, he fell ill, reputedly after a drinking bout, and died. The year was 323 B.C. and he was thirty-two years old.

Amidst all these world-transforming events in which Athens, Demosthenes notwithstanding, played little more than a passing part, Menander grew up in a city that could still consider itself the intellectual and cultural capital of the time. Plato was a man of middle age when Epaminondas defeated Sparta at Leuktra; in 342 Aristotle accepted from Philip the position of tutor to Alexander in Macedon; Theophrastus, Aristotle's successor as head of the Peripatetic School of philosophy in Athens, was old enough to be one of Menander's teachers, but much of his writing overlapped exactly with the years between 320 and 292 when Menander wrote all his plays.

The advent of Alexander, despite the protests of Demosthenes and his faction, had not been entirely bad for Athens. Its political power was gone forever, but the same was true for most of the city-states. Athens had simply had more warning than most. The leading statesmen of the Alexandrian period, Phokion and Lykurgus, were men of a different breed. Lykurgus who, either in his own name or through appointees and relatives, controlled public building between 338 and 326, inaugurated several programs that, among other things, bore directly on the theatre. Indeed, as we shall see later, the first permanent stone theatre in the precinct of Dionysus bears his name.

The comparative calm was illusory. One Harpalus, Alexander's treasurer, who already had a record of peculation, suddenly appeared in 324 off the coast of Athens. Harpalus had absconded with the Persian coffers, the spoil of conquest that Alexander had entrusted to his keeping during his prolonged absence in Arabia. Following a period of gaudy living in the Middle East, he saw the wisdom of withdrawing before Alexander's threatened return. Now he had arrived with money, ships, and mercenaries and endeavored to protect himself by inciting an anti-Macedonian revolt.

Harpalus' presence reawoke and exacerbated latent Athenian tensions. To receive him or reject him? To use him as a figurehead of independence or hand him over to Alexander? As so often in their history, the Athenians could not make up their minds. In the subsequent imbroglio Harpalus was killed, but much of his stolen money was discovered to be missing. Demosthenes, the outstanding orator of his time and Alexander's old opponent, made a convenient scapegoat. He was accused of complicity with Harpalus and suspected at least of carelessness, at worst of misappropriation. Tried and found guilty by his fellow Athenians, he was sentenced to imprisonment but soon found an opportunity to escape.

The Harpalus incident, though sensational in itself, was merely a harbinger of further turmoil. A year later came the report of Alexander's death. Throughout the country cities took the news as license to regain their independence. In the event it proved too late for that: the days of the city-state were over. Antipater, the late king's regent, marched southward with a punitive army out of Macedon. A comparatively unbloody engagement at Krannon in September of 322 proved as significant in its way as had Leuktra or Chaironeia, and any fond illusions about a return to a time of Athenian military might were rudely shattered. Antipater, former regent of Alexander in Macedon, took control of Athens, backed by the presence of a powerful Macedonian garrison based at Munychia. Demosthenes committed suicide as the leaders of the anti-Macedonian faction were systematically rooted out.

A number of histories of the Greek world choose to use the death of Alexander in 323 B.C., or the battle of Krannon in 322 as termini, particularly as Aristotle died in the same period. For some, it seems, most of what was interesting in Athenian life and civilization ended there.[2] The fact that the first performance of any of Menander's plays, *Orge* (*Anger*), may well have occurred at the Great Dionysia between the two events is incidental but tends to brand Menander as marking the end rather than the beginning of an era, the one playwright of repute who coincided exactly with the subjugation of the Athenian people. This is unfortunate because his achievement was never likely to be noted for patterning the political events of his career. Nevertheless, the decline in Athenian fortunes is undeniable.

One reason for treating Krannon as a conclusion was the subsequent dismantling of democracy in Athens, affecting the composition of theatre audiences by including the abolition of the theoric fund to subsidize tickets. There had been movements in the past to abandon the democratic system in favor of the propertied classes, notably after the end of the Peloponnesian War, but all had been abortive or short-lived. Now, for the first time since before Aeschylus' *Oresteia* in 458 B.C., the vote was restricted according to wealth. Twelve thousand of the poorer citizens who failed to qualify were banished. Conspiracies and counter-conspiracies rumbled on up until 311, with various factions claiming to have restored democracy by decree without having the teeth to put such decrees into action.

Antipater's death in 319 led, after two uncertain years, to a remarkable ten years until 307 with Athens under the control of a Macedonian-imposed regent, Demetrius of Phaleron, who was not only an Athenian but also a man of letters, a friend of both Aristotle and Theophrastus. Demetrius was something of an enlightened despot, a man of whose views Plato might well have approved. He maintained peace at the expense of democracy, believing that power should not be entrusted to the masses but be retained in the hands of a few trained experts. Under his guidance Athens certainly enjoyed a period of comparative peace and security at home. A disinterest in, even distaste for, public affairs became fashionable as fewer individuals saw reason to become involved in any aspect of public life. The disinclination of Menander's characters to be involved in other than domestic affairs may have been in part pragmatism on the part of the playwright, who enjoyed Demetrius' protection and patronage, but it was no less a mark of the times: comedy, as it had in the time of Aristophanes, still provided an indicator of public engagement. This Demetrius was eventually replaced by another Demetrius, known as Poliorketes, "the besieger of cities." In his hands Athens returned to a more ostensibly democratic constitution, though people's rights were never to be restored to a level that Perikles would have recognized.

The new Demetrius might well have posed a threat to such a close friend of the former Demetrius as Menander had been. One of the earliest new laws to be passed, introduced, ironically, by one Sokrates, aimed at suppressing the old philosophical schools and forbade the establishment of any new ones. Theophrastus was the likely target in his role as head of the

Peripatetics and a known confidant of Demetrius of Phaleron. Theophrastus left Athens but was back within a few months. The law had proved illegal, and anyway the Athenians were not sure how keen they were to disinherit themselves from their philosophical legacy simply on the grounds that Plato, Aristotle, and Theophrastus had little good to say about democracy. Athens learned to turn a blind eye.

Other cities fared worse. Corinth in particular was in turmoil for many years, having to endure its own Macedonian garrison and being threatened by one or another of Alexander's successors. These troublesome times affected the lives of all Athenians: yet in no play of Menander is there the slightest indication of what is happening in the real world outside the play. Even *The Shield* (*Aspis*), which is concerned with the assumed demise of a mercenary, concocts circumstances that seem to be invented rather than based on any actual war. Menander's plays barely hint at any political issue.

The remainder of Menander's life was lived out in circumstances where little occurred of consequence. The most momentous changes had come to pass almost subliminally, though they imbue Menander's work and give it its true Hellenistic flavor. The real revolution was an economic one. Trade, whose seasonal nature contributed to the isolation of the city-states, had become year-round as a result of improvements in ship design and increased incentives to merchants. Bankers became the new oracles, and there is nothing odd about a plot based, as is that of *The Woman from Samos*, on the absence of a merchant and his friend for the best part of a year up in the Black Sea. Pan and Chance are the gods who matter in Menander, not Apollo and Athene.

A comedy by Aristophanes is like a daily newspaper. However fantastic the plot, it also serves as a vivid and comprehensive survey of current events. Amidst the trivia and the gossip, the storms in teacups and the name-dropping, Aristophanes' characters, whether mythical, fictional, or real, are in and among the major issues of the day. Nor does he shirk from condemning the greatest of these issues, the war against Sparta. This abundance of information is one reason why later scholars sought to preserve Aristophanes' plays. They provide a record of fifth-century Athenian society unequaled by any other source.

One looks in vain for such commentary in Menander. It is true that *The Shorn Girl* goes against convention by being set in Corinth, rather than in Athens, perhaps in acknowledgment of that city's topical importance and the trouble there; and that one of the principal characters in that play is a military man of precisely the type that the post-Alexander dissensions had brought into prominence. For the most part, however, Menander's comedies tell us as little about the contemporary political situation as Sheridan's about the American Revolution or Coward's about the rise of European fascism in the 1930s. Such silence is significant. It shows that the Greeks had arrived at a new concept of what the theatre was for. In the midst of all the excitement surrounding him Menander prefers to concentrate on matters of Athenian domesticity where the only wars are family squabbles and the capture of a wife is more important than the winning of an empire. What is less clear is whether this reflects contemporary preference or is the product of a negative pressure on the theatre and the playwrights who wrote for it.[3]

History is as silent about Menander's private life as Menander is about history. We have a scattering of dates and a handful of rumors and conjecture. His father was Diopeithes of Kephisia. His uncle, it was once believed, was the playwright Alexis, whose comedies—over two hundred of them— had been a feature of the Athenian theatre for many years after the death of Aristophanes. This family connection no longer seems as certain as it once did, and the lack of any complete or even partially complete play between Aristophanes and Menander makes this whole area a somewhat fruitless one for speculation.

About Menander's education we can be more sure. Athens still housed philosophical schools that were justly famous and widely influential, although their emphasis had changed considerably. Such schools were, for the Greeks, the equivalent of our modern university education. We might think of them as graduate institutes devoted to particular lines of inquiry. They clustered around prominent figures, offering work in disciplines far beyond what we would now narrowly define as philosophy: conspicuously, in the art of public speaking, which in a city run by assemblies and committees, was essential for political and social advancement and as necessary to the Greeks as reading and writing are to us.

In the earlier part of the fourth century, philosophy in Athens had been dominated by Plato, pupil and apologist of Sokrates. Plato's long and influential work, *The Republic*, dealt with the composition of the ideal state. In practical politics and education he revealed himself as considerably less successful. In 367 B.C., his place was taken by Aristotle, whose family—a sign of the times—were court physicians to the royal house of Macedonia. Some years after serving as tutor to Alexander the Great in Pella, Aristotle returned to Athens, establishing his own school, the Lyceum, where he taught until 323. His retirement and death shortly afterward, coincided with the death of his famous ex-pupil.

Less concerned with the ideal than with the actual, Aristotle applied his natural inclination toward scientific inquiry to a wide range of disciplines.

He wrote treatises on politics and physics; on metaphysics, ethics, and rhetoric; and on the art of dramatic composition in the *Poetics*, one of the founding documents of dramatic aesthetics. In his turn, he was succeeded by Theophrastus, whose presence provided some continuity of teaching. There is a tradition that Theophrastus had heard Plato lecture. This means that he must have come to Athens as a young man before he was twenty-three. He stayed to work with Aristotle, probably accompanied him on his travels, and was with him at the Lyceum. When Aristotle left Athens shortly before his death, Theophrastus took over the school and ensured the continuity of his master's teaching and research until his own death thirty-five years later.

Menander, as we have noted, became one of Theophrastus' pupils: so did Demetrius of Phaleron, the future Macedonian viceroy of Athens. Theophrastus was a distinguished figure in his own right but, like Sokrates and Plato before him, he fell victim to the vicious infighting of Greek politics. At one point in his career he was put on trial for impiety (a useful blanket charge, similar to that used a century before to entrap Sokrates), but he, unlike Sokrates, was acquitted. Menander himself is said to have been in some danger through his political connections. This in itself, or at least the kind of official approval he enjoyed, may well have been a reason for his reluctance to give his plays any contemporary slant.

Classical tradition wove a romantic story around Menander, assigning him a mistress, one Glykera, who was believed to be portrayed with him on a stone relief showing the playwright with some of his typical masks.[4] The playwright communing with his Muse seems as plausible an interpretation of the scene. Beyond this, our personal information is scanty. Menander died at the age of fifty-two, according to one story by drowning in the Athenian harbor of Piraeus.[5]

We can be more positive in describing the city that he lived and worked in. In many ways Menander's Athens was a diminished city, overshadowed by its own glorious past. Admittedly, the city had risen above the economic depression following defeat by Sparta. The destruction of the long walls had been a brand of shame, but these walls were now rebuilt. Athens had even come close, once or twice, to reestablishing itself as the center of a confederacy, though to nothing like the extent of its former empire.

By the time of Krannon, however, even the diehards recognized that political supremacy was a thing of the past. Athens, like other communities across the new, larger Greek world, submitted to a common administration that eroded the abrasive differences between them. The Hellenistic age was a blander and more homogeneous and more secular one, with administrative buildings replacing temples of the local gods as the city's nerve center.

Athenian prestige was maintained by the city's continuing cultural authority. In the fifth century, artistic eminence had gone hand in hand with political supremacy. Although other cities developed their own schools of poetry, sculpture, and painting, they came more and more to be judged by Athenian standards. In literature Athenian works are often the only ones to have survived. In drama this was wholly true. Although we talk of "Greek theatre," the body of plays we possess is uniqely Athenian.

Even the language of the Hellenistic world derived from this source. Greek became the official tongue throughout Alexander's conquests, and its basis was the distinctive Athenian dialect. *Koine*, as it came to be called, "the common language," was simplified Attic-Ionic, shorn of its grammatical idiosyncrasies and made more accessible to foreign speakers. It bore the same relationship to the mother tongue as the English, say, of India under the British *Raj*. In time, it would become the Greek of the New Testament.

Menander's plays display an awareness of these linguistic changes. Aristophanes' comedies burst with local pride and speak to an Athenian public in their own accent. Menander's work is aimed at a broader, international audience. His language is milder, less aggressive. He does not, like Aristophanes, twist words or invent them. His verse—and it is still verse, however colloquial, mainly in the iambic meter that drama had claimed as its own—is milder to the ear, less abrasive in tone, catching the gentler rhythms of everyday conversation. Though still patterned language whose dramatic artifice is evident, it moves closer to the real world. More remarkably, the language is the language of the characters, fashioned and shaped to reveal them as individuals in a way that happens rarely in other Greek playwrights, even Euripides. Mellifluous and lifting, easy to the tongue and the ear, it does not achieve Aristophanes' heights and does not seek them. The chief difficulty in translating Aristophanes is to convey his brilliance and verbal felicity in so comparatively clumsy a language as English. In Menander, it is to restrain the verse from falling into the flatness of naturalistic as opposed to dramatic prose while hinting at the range of undercurrents beneath the surface of a deceptively simple dialogue.

The continuance of Athenian traditions was furthered by one of Alexander's most successful creations. In his tour of conquest, he had founded a number of new cities bearing his own name. The most prominent of these, Alexandria in Egypt, contained a library and museum that became the intellectual center of the Hellenistic world. Its curators sought material from all sources and in many languages, building up an unequaled collection. Many of the works were important scientific treatises, drawn from pre-Greek cultures and, since the destruction of the library, lost to us. But the arts had a proud place also. The librarians paid particular attention to the masterpieces of fifth-century Athens, copying, collecting, and annotating them. Texts were created here which circulated round the world as schoolbooks and from them derive, in many cases, the texts that we still have. Thus Alexandria perpetuated the cultural influence of a city that had lost political power of its own.

To point to the cultural significance of Alexandria within the Hellenistic world is to characterize the age. It was not only in Athens that the fourth century looked back with nostalgia to the fifth. This was an age more concerned with remembering the past than with emulating it. The leading lights of Alexandria were scholars, compilers, and recorders. They were not men of creative genius. In the fifth century, the characteristic literary utterance is the poem. In the Hellenistic period it becomes the dictionary.

Such original writers as there were achieved only qualified success. The world has lost their works or forgotten them. Together with the expansion of Greek territory had come a dilution of quality. Artistically, the new world lacked the vitality and impetus of the old. Too often the new arts were merely imitative. Writers confined themselves within the traditional genres, content to restate—though often with greater elaboration—what had already been said. Just as *koine* represents a watered-down Athenian dialect, so, for the most part, Hellenistic art and literature are second-hand versions of their fifth-century counterparts, concerned more with technical virtuosity than with content.

Among the Hellenistic arts, the theatre did offer some evidence of an original sense of purpose. Since the first tentative appearances of drama as a feature of public life, plays had traditionally been confined to festivals held for a limited duration only. In the fifth century the major dramatic festivals had been Athenian. In this respect, as in so many others, we see an Athens-dominated culture. Although other cities, both great and small, constructed theatres, it was the Athenian playwrights who were invited to display their work in other centers. For all practical purposes Greek drama as we know it was an essentially Athenian art, performed as part of two major festivals held annually in winter and early spring, with some additional local manifestations of a rudimentary "straw-hat circuit."

The principal Athenian festivals continued throughout the Hellenistic period and for long after. Although their religious and civic functions were gradually eroded, they survived as artistic enterprises hallowed by tradition and antiquity. Menander was heir to this tradition and, like Aristophanes before him, submitted works for performance at these celebrations in his home city.

By Menander's time, however, the nature of the theatre as a profession had changed in a way that Aristophanes would hardly have recognized. In the first half of the fifth century, the theatre had been an amateur, or at most a semiprofessional, activity. Playwrights could not expect to earn a living from their plays. They were men of substance or engaged in other activities, for whom playwriting was simply one of several interests, another way of contributing to the rich and diverse pattern of city life.

Similarly, actors could not expect to make a full-time living out of acting. The opportunities did not yet exist. There was no such thing as a long run in the Athenian theatre. Plays could expect no more than a single festival performance in the author's lifetime, and appearances outside Athens were of minor importance and limited. Once their festival fee had been paid, therefore, actors had to seek other work for most of the year. There is ample evidence that a number of them applied their stage skills to the teaching of public speaking, one of the essential arts of the time and one they were particularly qualified to practice.

In the fourth century, however, a new professionalism began to manifest itself in the Greek theatre. Opportunities for performance multiplied as individual Greek communities away from the main centers began to take on board and ape the metropolitan cultures. Plays were no longer confined to a few festivals in the major cities of mainland Greece but began to be offered whenever and wherever a paying audience could be found. Patronal festivals could happen at any time of the year, and the performing calendar was extended accordingly.[6]

Recognizing this, actors began to form touring companies, which was made easier by the economy of means that has always characterized Greek drama. Convenience and tradition had limited the number of actors required to perform most tragedies as long as the Chorus were separately rehearsed. Touring companies took with them their own musician, thus raising the personnel to four, and relied on whoever had hired their services to supply whatever else was needed that they could not carry with them. The similar spatial relationships and scenic capabilities of most fourth-century and Hellenistic theatre buildings made the process of adaptation much more straightforward than most modern touring companies are likely to face.

It did not take long for the process to become highly professional with guilds of actors offering a guarantee of quality and, eventually, a guarantee of appearance with fines or other sanctions imposed on those incompetents or unfortunates for whom the vicissitudes of travel in the ancient world had proved insurmountable. Major city festivals were soon to hire in productions on a similar basis with the leading actors arriving, much as do many of today's opera singers, into a pre-rehearsed production. The orator Aeschines, Demosthenes' principal opponent in the Macedonian debate, had worked as one of just such a three-actor company, offering adapted touring versions of fifth-century works in local theatres, before changing professions and taking up politics.

This new professionalism enlarged the scope of the theatre and brought it to wider audiences. With Alexander's conquests, these audiences were immeasurably increased. Actors of lesser standing, sensing new financial opportunities, followed in the wake of the armies apparently to the furthest limits. Technical terms of Greek origin appear in the earliest Sanskrit theatre. Quite small communities already had permanent stone theatres (many of them still survive) in which the visitors would play, but there was also a less formal circuit. Companies taking to the road without the surety of a contract might take their own theatres with them consisting of a platform and a curtained background: or they might rely for their simple stage, as strolling players after them customarily did, on the generosity of a local innkeeper whose business was certainly not harmed by sponsoring some outside entertainment, however rough. We have pictorial evidence for basic cloth and frame settings from reliefs and vase-paintings, notably from southern Italy.[7] The performances seem to relate minimally to the classical repertoire of Sophocles or Euripides, although the connections between the farcical fare of the traveling troupes and the satyr plays, which from earliest times had concluded a diet of tragedy in the Theatre of Dionysus in Athens, may have been much closer than is usually assumed.

Actors, legitimate or casual, had become gypsies. The "cart of Thespis," which features in the earliest legend of dramatic performance, maintains a more solid and unbroken tradition of theatre than the permanent playhouse ever managed. What the stage gained in mobility, however, it lost in reputation. Fifth-century actors had been hung with honors, the means by which the Athenian playwright could offer an Athenian message to his fellow Athenians. Actors in Athens had been regarded as the central figures in some of the state's most important collective functions, given a quasi-priestly coloration by the rites in which they participated. This importance may have carried into other areas of public life. They were later selected to speak for the community, to act as delegates or ambassadors in acknowledgment of their recognized communications skills.

In the regular festivals of mainland Greece, some of these associations persisted. The traveling performer, however, was well on the way to becoming the pariah that Plato considered his just desert, a restless chameleon pursuing a skill that was admirable in its own way but somehow suspect when adopted as a profession. Aristotle, a defender of the drama, laments in the *Poetics* that the theatre, which had once belonged to the playwrights, had in his time fallen into the hands of the actors. He inquires plaintively why the artists of Dionysus—actors—always seem to be men of dubious moral character. It was from an awareness of their vulnerability that the more responsible actors began to form themselves into protective associations. As G. M. Sifakis shows, a rudimentary form of Actors' Equity dates from the first of the Guilds. The Artists of Dionysus had its headquarters on the island of Delos, the legendary birthplace of Apollo, and, like its modern counterpart, it sought to protect the well-being of its members by setting standards and supervising contracts on the one hand and protecting the players from exploitation on the other.

If actors were in one sense diminished by going on the road, the reputation of individuals could grow rapidly. Fame, for which all their fellows before and since have so strenuously striven, led to the emergence of a star system that the earlier period had never known. In the fifth century we know little about individual actors. Some names survive but are mostly subordinate to the playwrights in whose works they appeared. The festivals had always awarded prizes to the poet whose work was judged best. In 449 B.C., these had been augmented by a new award, specifically for the best actor. This innovation suggests that actors were now beginning to be regarded—perhaps to insist on being regarded—as creative artists in their own right and not merely as mouthpieces of the poet. It also coincides with the passing of the era in which the playwright was automatically regarded as lead actor. In the fourth century not only do we have more names, but we also know more about actors as individuals. They display powerful personalities in their own right, often adapting existing material to their own talents or exploiting their own mannerisms and idiosyncrasies.

The staple of the fifth-century theatre had been tragedy. This was the first dramatic form to make a festival appearance, retaining its hold on the Athenian public by using legendary material to pose socially relevant questions. Tragedy was a recognized focus of public discussion and the most public and powerful medium for the consideration of contemporary issues. Comedy—though in Aristophanes' hand no less socially and politically involved—was a comparative latecomer to the Great Dionysia and admitted only to secondary status in the major festivals.

The early part of the fourth century seemed to reinforce this priority, but tragedy fell victim to a lack of originality. The festivals welcomed the revival of the fifth-century masters, Euripides above the rest, but the newer playwrights were unable to find a personal path. Some attempt was made to widen the scope of tragedy with forays into plays from contemporary history, but for the most part the fourth-century tragedians rang the changes on the old stories with less and less probable variations. Astydamas' *Antigone*, a prizewinner in 341, seems to have jumbled up a host of former myths in his tale of a son of Antigone and Haemon hidden away among shepherds and recognized as a grown-up by a birthmark when he returns to Thebes.

If Sophocles might have winced at that, what might Euripides have made of Karkinos' *Medea* where Medea is accused of the murder of her children but claims she simply sent them away into safety because it would have been foolish to kill her children while leaving Jason alive? Despite an apparent taste for sensation, the newer tragedy really reveals a paucity of vision. Originality came with the work of the comedians like Alexis and Antiphanes for whom the impossibility of aping Aristophanes opened up instead the domestic world.

Middle Comedy, the transitional form between Old Comedy and New, has proved so difficult to define that some critics would say that it scarcely deserves to exist in a separate category and that all Greek comedy was either "Old" or "New."[8] As we saw earlier, it is represented by two late plays of Aristophanes from the early part of the fourth century and a mass of names and quotations from the following seventy years. However one chooses to classify, and all such categorizing of genres is no more than a matter of convenience for later generations, the last years of the century saw the real rise of New Comedy. This comprised the works of Menander himself, his contemporaries and imitators, including the Latin playwrights of the late third and second centuries, Plautus and Terence. New Comedy, as we have seen, was popular and widely influential.

Critics attempting to come to grips with the original elements of New Comedy were baffled for a long time by the lack of proper source material. Menander was obviously in demand in his own time and was used as a term of reference after his death. A hundred plays were attributed to him, far more than could have been consumed by the Athenian festivals. He must either have been writing for other places and other companies, or he was a victim, as Plautus later, of authorial piracy. Even in Shakespeare's time, the successful playwright had scant defense against the unscrupulous theatre manager who would use a successful dramatist's name to sell inferior work.

Nevertheless, Menander's reputation in antiquity was extraordinary. Thirty years after his death, a later Aristophanes, the scholar of Byzantium, uttered his famous paean to realism: "O life and Menander! Which of you imitated the other?"[9] and decided he was second only to Homer among ancient poets. Julius Caesar, using Menander as his comic yardstick, found Terence only half as good.[10] Plutarch, who wrote an essay comparing him with Aristophanes, asked why anyone would go to the theatre except to see Menander.[11] Given this popularity, it was extraordinary that none of the works seemed to have survived. It is significant, perhaps, that scholarship did not see fit to catalogue the Menandrian corpus. Selected plays by Aeschylus, Sophocles, and Euripides were preserved in the Athenian archives as well as in the library of Alexandria. The dignity and nobility of tragedy enhanced by time had made them museum pieces to be studied for edification rather than immediate theatrical enjoyment. Aristophanes the playwright was also preserved but almost by accident as a repository of intimate data about a vanished way of life.

Menander appealed to other writers but apparently did not have the same claim on critical attention. He had written to highlight human foibles rather than contribute to any contemporary political or philosophical debate. He was part of the working theatre, aiming to edify through entertainment. Prized though they were by audiences and other writers, Menander's plays failed to speak as the representatives of a noble culture. They lacked the antiquarian associations that justified the preservation of their predecessors. The story, if true, of Terence's drowning while on a mission to Greece to collect more manuscripts of Menander is doubly significant. Menander was important enough to be searched for, but much of his work, even after so short space of time, was no longer immediately accessible.

The mystery is that, whatever Aristophanes of Byzantium thought, or Julius Caesar, or any of the others who later bestowed such extravagant praise, when Menander vanished from the performing tradition, his works apparently vanished too. Obviously, there were copies in libraries or private collections, but they were not generally available in Rome. Before too harsh a verdict is passed on the scholars and literary critics, it is worth recalling what a tiny proportion of all Greek comedy and tragedy did survive: perhaps 8 percent of Aeschylus or Sophocles and nothing at all, apart from Euripides, of the hundreds of their contemporaries who wrote, presented, and won prizes for their plays in Athens for the best part of two hundred years. Old Comedy is nine plays of Aristophanes, and Middle Comedy, if it exists, two. That New Comedy in Greek amounted to not a single play was disappointing but not a complete surprise. There was simply a break in the scholarly tradition.

Up to and including the nineteenth century, critics who wished to evaluate Menander could do so only at second hand by recourse to his Roman imitators. Here there was at least ample material. Plautus (c. 250–184 B.C.) left us twenty complete plays and fragments of one other, Terence left six, his complete output. All these works may be said to benefit from the influence of Menander, some more explicitly than others. The question was, how much? The consensus of scholarship was that Plautus had tailored his originals to suit a less refined audience, while Terence was more of a purist. But Terence himself admitted to combining Greek originals to make a new Roman play.

The general tendencies of Greek New Comedy were clear. The plays were comedies of manners, devoid of political comment and revolving around universally comprehensible domestic situations. They involved stereotypical characters representing various classes of society. But the question of how much was Menander and how much his imitator, how much represented the Hellenistic spirit and how much the grafting on of later Roman attitudes, developed into an elegant scholarly game in which each Roman play was subjected to intense scrutiny to determine where the *urdrama* ended and the embellishment began.

It was not until the beginning of the twentieth century that the gaps began to be filled. Some fragments had been found sewn inside another manuscript in a monastery on Mount Sinai in 1844, but they were tiny pieces. Egypt was to prove more fruitful. The preservation of manuscripts there has been the result of a combination of climate and geography. Papyrus is a highly perishable material. In Greece the weather is wet enough for it to be unlikely to survive. In the drier climate of Egypt the chances were better. So in Egypt in 1905 French archaeologist Gustave Lefebvre discovered in a jar what is known to scholars as the *Cairo Codex*, containing the remains of what had been five complete plays, *The Woman from Samos (Samia)*, *The Arbitration (Epitrepontes)*, *The Shorn Girl (Perikeiromene)*, *The Hero (Heros)*, and one other whose title had not been verified. Although none of these plays was intact, Menander was at least partially restored from oblivion. Some of the fragments were long enough to allow the plot to be reconstructed, if imperfectly.

The Cairo manuscript was followed by other discoveries, notably the publication in 1957 of a codex in the possession of Swiss bibliophile Martin Bodmer with, for the first time, one of Menander's comedies virtually complete. This was the *Duskolos*, translated variously as *The Bad-Tempered*

Man, The Grouch, The Peevish Fellow, Old Cantankerous, The Man Who Hated People,[12] or *The Malcontent*.[13]

The Bodmer papyrus, which dates from the third century A.D., also contained substantial portions of *The Shield* (*Aspis*) and enough of *The Woman from Samos* for us now to treat it, with reservations, as a complete play. This part of the manuscript had to wait until 1969 for publication.

Between these two dates, other discoveries were surfacing. One, in particular, shows how haphazard the whole process can be, but it also gives hope that our knowledge of Menander may not yet be complete. In 1964 two papyrologists working at the Sorbonne in Paris, A. Blanchard and R. Bataille, revealed that some glued sheets of papyrus used to wrap Egyptian mummies were actually part of a third century B.C. text of Menander's *The Sikyonian* (*Sikuonios*). Five hundred lines of a barely known play have now been recovered.

Not surprisingly, when in 1957 the first complete play finally saw the light of day, scholars fell upon it with avidity. *The Malcontent* was after all the first new classical play to be discovered in its entirety since the reappearance of some lost plays of Plautus in the Renaissance. The first English translation appeared in the journal *Horizon* as a literary scoop by Gilbert Highet who completed it in a matter of a few weeks. Eight other English translations appeared in the first year, indeed one from South Africa. The play's first performance in over two thousand years was staged in Geneva in French. It was soon to be performed in modern Greek at the Epidaurus Festival and in ancient Greek at King's College in the University of London. And scholarly articles proliferated.

Most of these articles were concerned with textual matters. Although we call *The Malcontent* complete, it is not properly speaking so. There are small gaps in the manuscript, and individual words, phrases, and even the attribution of lines to specific characters are in doubt. The intricate labor of restoring the original text still goes on.

The wave of interest in the text, however, was hardly matched by critical response to the play as a play. The general reaction was one of disappointment. Here, it seemed, was a dramatist whose reputation had become so inflated by antiquity that the plays, when they finally reappeared, were almost bound to be an anticlimax.

The reception accorded to the first discoveries in the Cairo Codex had been less than enthusiastic. For example, Francis G. Allinson, in his preface to the first collected edition published in the Loeb Classical Library, stated:

The traditional estimate of his plays, verifiable only by numerous minor fragments and by the uncertain reflection in Roman Comedy, had become so firmly embedded in our literary creed that the opportunity for a more independent opinion, based upon recent discoveries of manuscripts, has entailed an excessive reaction in the minds of some competent critics. This was, perhaps, inevitable. Exaggerated or uncritical praise provokes unmerited depreciation.[14]

So also, more unkindly, was W. Tarn's summing up of the dramatic achievement of the period in his survey of Hellenistic civilization first published in 1927:

> (Menander) and his imitators seem about the dreariest desert in literature. Life is not entirely composed of seductions and unwanted children, coincidence and recognitions of long-lost daughters, irate fathers and impertinent slaves. Doubtless he had met these things; but though his characters were types, the life was not typical.[15]

When, in 1957, one whole play came to light and in 1969, almost all of another with substantial sections of a third, it at least became possible to have something tangible to review.

What seemed at first most perplexing was the ancient perception of Menander's realism. The Greeks obviously considered his plays to be a mirror of life: to us they often seem hardly realistic at all. Many of his characters, it is argued, are stereotypes, behaving according to predetermined modes that have more to do with literary convention than with observation of human psychology. The situations, as in Tarn's critique, are seen to be limited in extent, fanciful in nature, and lacking true social relevance. The motivations arise not from the wellsprings of human behavior but from arbitrary contrivance; the characters move adroitly enough, but, like pieces on a board, they are controlled by their unseen manipulator.

To these and similar criticisms two immediate responses may be made. First, Menander's plays, like most comedies, lose much of their impact when they are merely read, not acted. Reading tragedy may lose a dimension that only performance can supply, but the cultivated reader can gain a fair impression of the play's dynamic. Comedy needs the emphasis, the timing, the sense of the line delivered and of stage picture to make full sense. These plays appear to work as vehicles for actors in a manner that should return them to the world's repertoire.

Second, Menander created a tradition that has grown and developed over two millennia. Devices that were fresh and innovative with him have become familiar in intimate comedy though they were created for performance in a masked tradition. That tradition is one that is rarer today, though happily one that has enjoyed its own renaissance in the twentieth century in the work of a number of theatrical directors from Vsevolod Meyerhold to Giorgio Strehler and in the recent smaller scale work of a whole host of improvisational companies whose immediate influence is the *commedia dell'arte*. Such a tradition can easily accommodate both stereotypical and subtle behavior.

Those responses are, I would submit, defensive ones. Menander offers more than this. It is in the handling of major relationships that Menander's dramatic bite and his capacity for the unexpected transcend the centuries. As actors will find, the fabled realism is built on a Chekhovian capacity for the unexpressed that fully accounts for his audiences finding characters both sharply drawn and realistic. Superficially, Menander's characters may seem routine. We would be as wrong to consider them so as to consider routine the writers, actresses, doctor, and bailiff of Chekhov's *Seagull*. This is something to which I will return in Chapter 6.

With effectively two whole plays and several large sections to work on, we are now in a position to see that Allinson and Tarn's earlier verdicts of were at best premature. To arrive at a better assessment of Menander as a maker of plays, we need to make something of an imaginative transposition: to put ourselves back into his time and come to terms with the values of the society he portrayed. At the same time, we need to apply a fine dramatic understanding to the way in which any subtle play is crafted by a playmaker as skilled as Menander. The most revealing story of his method is of the friend who asked if he had yet finished his play and received the reply: "Yes, it's complete. All I have to do is write it."[16] That is a playmaker's answer.

A number of factors and conventions contributed to the performance of the original plays in the fourth and third centuries B.C.—stage conditions, the theatre for which they were originally intended, the audience, and the occasion. To these we must now turn.

NOTES

1. See Edith Hall, *Inventing the Barbarian: Greek Self-Definition Through Tragedy*, Oxford: Clarendon Press, 1989.

2. Peter Green, on the other hand, takes the funeral games for Alexander in 323 B.C. as the starting point for his monumental *Alexander to Actium*, Los Angeles: University of California Press, 1990.

3. T.B.L. Webster rehearses a complete catalogue of possible contemporary references within the plays in his *An Introduction to Menander*, Manchester: Manchester University Press, 1974.

4. See W. G. Arnott, *Menander I*, Cambridge, Mass. and London: Heine-mann and Harvard University Press, 1973, pp. xvi–xvii.

5. A similar story would be told of Latin playwright Terence, apparently on a mission to discover lost Menander manuscripts.

6. For details of the Guilds and their records, see G. M. Sifakis, *Studies in the History of Hellenistic Drama*, London: Athlone Press, 1967.

7. The most comprehensive collection of such illustrations is to be found in A. D. Trendall and T.B.L. Webster's *Illustrations of Greek Drama*, London: Phaidon Press, 1971. See also O. Taplin, *Comic Angels*, Oxford: Oxford University Press, 1993, for the significance of southern Italian vase-painting in the reconstruction of theatre history; and H. A. Shapiro, *Myth into Art*, London and New York: Routledge, 1994.

8. I confess to doing the same in the Methuen volume *Aristophanes and Menander: New Comedy*, London: Methuen, 1994, which includes the Menander translations used in the present volume.

9. On Syrianus *Hermogenes*, 2, 23.

10. But see G. E. Duckworth, *The Nature of Roman Comedy*, Princeton, N.J.: Princeton University Press, 1952, p. 385, note 4, who doubts the story's reliability.

11. See Appendix 1.

12. Peter Arnott's title for the 1990 production for the Tufts Avenue Theatre. See Appendix 2.

13. My own published translation from which all quotations in this book are taken.

14. F. G. Allinson, *Menander*, London and New York: Heinemann and Harvard University Press, 1921, pp. ix–x.

15. W. Tarn and G. T. Griffith, *Hellenistic Civilisation*, 3rd ed., London: Edward Arnold, 1952, p. 273: a verdict somewhat sourly endorsed by Peter Green in *Alexander to Actium*, pp. 65–79.

16. Quoted in Plutarch, *Moralia*, 347 f.

Chapter 3

Theatre and Society

One of the most impressive discoveries of twentieth-century archaeology has been, not the excavation of some long-vanished site, or even the discovery of some hitherto unknown culture, but the reconstruction of the ancient trireme. After centuries of speculation, the original design has been established and a replica built. Manned by a hand-picked and finely trained crew, it has come close to reaching ancient speeds. The vessel on which Athens depended for command of the seas, economic and political ascendancy, sails again. One consequence of this experiment has been to affirm the aptness of the most pervasive of Greek metaphors "the ship of state." It is now fully apparent why the Athenians so frequently equated their democracy with their navy. In a trireme there can be no passengers. The three banks of oars must operate with immaculate precision. It takes only one oarsman fouling a stroke to cause havoc and bring the voyage to a halt. The efficiency of the ship is the efficiency of each and every member of the crew: hence, the wholesale freeing of the slaves who rowed in the battle of Arginusai in 406 B.C. to which Aristophanes bears witness in *Frogs*.

Arnott's parallel between what was effectively the engine of Athenian power in the time of Aristophanes, the warship, and the processes of democracy as demonstrated by individual responsibility may be matched, if not by a similar image, at least by an intriguing transition in the wake of the conquests of Alexander. The fifth century had promulgated the notion of the inferiority of all races other than Greek. If the Athenians, the Spartans no less, had been convinced of the superiority of their own systems, we can find abundant evidence in the liberal Euripides of the incidence of rampant racial prejudice.[1] As in later colonial manifestations in centuries closer to our own, such prejudice was to survive long after the notional political justification for it had disappeared as surely as does the phantom Helen in Euripides' comedy that bears her name. Aristotle was still fostering the belief in the superiority of the Greeks at a time when the rise of Macedon was demonstrating how tenuous such a claim might be. By the midpoint of Menander's career, a new idea was taking hold, a smaller, faster merchant-craft, if we want to pursue the sailing analogy, whose function was less to protect local waters within an existing sphere of influence than to reach out to the far corners of the known world.

Zeno established his school of Stoic philosophy in Athens only six years after the abortive attempt in 307 B.C. to outlaw the philosophers from Athens. A Cypriot, probably semitic in origin, Zeno seems to have arrived in Athens largely by accident. He was to continue to teach at the school he founded in 301 for the next forty years. His philosophy was to pose an alternate ideal state to that of Plato, seventy years before. Zeno picked up the idea of cosmopolitanism, which the Cynics used largely to justify an antipathy to affairs of state, and offer instead a new worldview. As J. B. Bury summed it up, "In the ideal state of Zeno all human beings were citizens."[2] The whole world was one's fatherland. Everyone could lay claims to being part of a single state, less a physical state, one feels, than a state of mind, anticipated, perhaps, by Menander when he shows the limitations of a man like Knemon in *The Malcontent* who wants to live his life cut off from as much human contact as possible.

If Menander's vision of the world and the place of the individual within that world had changed out of all recognition from the heyday of Athenian democracy, there were other areas of influence that had changed surprisingly little. Among these was an education system rooted in the power of the spoken word and what was claimed as reasoned argument.

During the fifth century attendance at the *Ekklesia*, the popular assembly, was a public obligation recognized by every right-minded citizen. The *Ekklesia* met on the Pnyx, a low hill across the valley from the Acropolis, in an open-air structure remarkably similar in its outlines to the theatre of Dionysus so close nearby. Aristophanes intuitively identified the complementary nature of theatre and Pnyx, of politics and drama. The same crowd that packed the auditorium for his comedies filled the *Ekklesia* for political debate: the same clientele in a similar spatial disposition. The history of fifth-century Athens is the history, for better or worse, of collective decisions. These decisions were molded by persuasive orators, thus rhetoric early became one of the cardinal educational disciplines, the key to advancement in public life.

The fondness for public participation was extended to the judicial system. Just as all citizens of the fifth century were expected to vote, so they were required to participate in the judicial process. Some major offenses were matters for the *Ekklesia*: minor misdemeanors could be dealt with in the equivalent of the County Court. But for the most part the legal system involved large numbers of people. No Athenian jury consisted merely of "twelve good men and true." A large enough section of the Athenian population enjoyed the whole process of the law for Aristophanes to base the whole of his *Wasps* on the local obsession. Several courts were unroofed and open to the sky. One recently excavated in the *Agora* could have held 1,500 members and more.[3]

Even the smaller juries were, by modern standards, huge; the minimum size was 201 men. When Sokrates stood trial in 399 B.C., he was brought before a jury of 501. Significantly, much of the finest and most important literature from the fourth century is the work of Demosthenes who became the foremost orator of his age by cultivating the art of persuasion in a number of celebrated court cases, often against the former actor, Aeschines. The law and the acting profession were ever linked, but the combined forces of Athenian contentiousness and devotion to argument were well matched in court and theatre. Notoriously litigious, the Athenians regarded the courts not merely as an element in the machinery of government but as part of the entertainment industry.

The enormous complexity and hazard involved in recourse to law, if not as fraught as pointed to by Dickens or Kafka, was sufficiently daunting to give rise to the process of arbitration by a single disinterested body. Such an incident figures largely as a dramatic device in New Comedy. Menander's *The Arbitration* (*Epitrepontes*) offers a fine example. About half of the play survives but enough for the eminent classicist Gilbert Murray to have felt justified in creating a play of his own from the fragments and presenting it as a legitimate piece of theatre in 1945.

The plot, as has been earlier remarked, has much in common with Euripides' *Ion*. Pamphile is a respectable Athenian girl who was raped by an unseen assailant after attending a women's festival. The only clue to the attacker is a ring that he dropped or she took from him. She became pregnant and was married a few months later to a young man called Charisios. She gives birth to the child while Charisios is away on business. The child is exposed but a slave tells Charisios the truth and he disowns his wife, setting up house instead with a whore called Habrotonon.

The child, of course, has been recovered, but a dispute ensues between Daos and Syros over the ownership of the trinkets that have been left with the baby. They appeal to a passer-by, who happens to be Pamphile's father:

SYROS: Please, sir, please could you spare us a moment?

SMIKRINES: Both of you? What's it about?

SYROS: We're having a disagreement.

SMIKRINES: What's it to do with me?

SYROS: We want an impartial third party. If there's nothing to stop you, could you serve as arbitrator?

SMIKRINES: Confound the pair of you. Wandering about, presenting cases and demanding justice.

SYROS: It's only a small matter, easy to understand. Please don't despise us, sir, for god's sake. It's in all our interests that justice should prevail, anywhere, the whole world over. And it's every man's duty to contribute and do his bit.

DAOS: The complete orator, this one. Why did I get involved?

SMIKRINES: Will you stick by my decision? Both of you?

SYROS: Absolutely. (*The Arbitration* 224–37)

The sequence is a device, part of a complicated dramatic process, to ensure that the ring which the rapist left behind is recognized as belonging to Charisios, the husband. Not only will the child prove legitimate, or near enough, but the young couple will be able to resume their relationship and live happily ever after. The dubious morality of such a tale will be considered later. For the present, what is significant is the means by which a legal matter is resolved without going to court by the involvement of a total stranger, who is inveigled into service as arbitrator on the grounds that it is his duty so to do. Here is an intriguing insight into a new age of personal concern.

It is in this context of a change from public to private involvement that we may consider the development of the theatre, for it reveals a similar impulse by way of the chorus. The chorus of Aristophanes had been as central to the comedy in the Theatre of Dionysus, as was the jury to the trial in the Heliaia. Greek tradition held that local choruses, celebrating gods, rulers, and events in song and dance, were one of the earliest precursors of the drama and one of its formative influences. Drama began, it has generally been agreed, when the first actor took on an identity other than his own to tell a story through the medium of a chorus.

The earliest comedies of Aristophanes show the chorus as an essential, indeed nuclear, component of the dramatic experience. With the passing of the years some curtailment of the chorus took place in tragedy as greater emphasis was placed on character and dramatic action, but up to *Women in Power* (*Ekklesiazousai*) and *Wealth* (*Ploutos*), the last two plays of Aristophanes, the chorus remained an active ingredient. In *Women in Power*, in which the women of Athens disguise themselves in their husbands' clothing to vote themselves into taking over the Assembly, the Chorus have a major responsibility in promoting the early part of the plot. However, they function largely as individuals and, as the strain of trying to cope with so many characters takes its toll, it would seem, on the playwright, the choral interlude is reduced to the stage direction, *chorou*, indicated in the text, followed immediately by the resumption of dialogue.[4]

Wealth sees a further diminution of their responsibility. In this last play, Aristophanes reflects the new mood of the drama in a treatment of his chorus which is almost perfunctory. They do not put in an appearance at all until the play is 250 lines old. Their involvement with the action then is negligible, and their first choral ode is once more a stage direction. The last five hundred lines offer two more such stage directions but not a single line of choral dialogue up to the final exit where they tie the play up with:

> It's time to go
> To close the show
> Dance after me.
> Right? One, two, three . . . (1205–1208, trans. Kenneth McLeish)

Little enough is known of the other playwrights of the early fourth century—Diphilus and Philemon seem to have enjoyed the greatest success—but their choruses too served only to provide intermezzi. Such a change deserves further examination.

Traditionally, the chorus had always been amateur, recruited from the citizen body, and there is no reason to believe that this was in any way affected by the other changes that the theatre underwent. The more professional the actors become it seems, the less important are the chorus. Plainly, the less integrated the chorus within the action, the easier for their rehearsal to be independent of the main action. Whether, as for juries, each tribe was expected to produce a quota of chorus members, or whether the enrollment cuts across such boundaries, we do not know. In general terms, however, we can see that, given the number of plays performed at the two major festivals of the Great Dionysia and the Lenaia, a considerable number of citizens would have been required each year. Public involvement must have been cumulative. Over the years a substantial proportion of the citizen body was drawn into the production of plays. By this means was created a sophisticated and informed audience, which was used to viewing the theatre as participants rather than merely as spectators. The theatre, no less than the *Ekklesia*, or the law-court, was a function of the public will. Any Athenian male (women as usual did not participate) might be a member of the chorus one year and a member of the audience the next. The familiarity created a bond between the public and performance which no later drama form has fully recreated. Even when the chorus ceased to be an element in the development of the plot and the actors achieved professional status, the majority of the performers were trained amateurs, performing to an audience of their peers. The play was the public on stage.

It is essential, then, to see the chorus not merely as a dramatic device but as the product of a particular social system. So often, the problems of reviving classic plays arise not from attempting to rediscover a lost theatrical style but from the impossibility of reconstructing a vanished society. That society, in the case of fifth century Athens, had been marvelously self-absorbed. The growth of theatrical traditions in other areas of Greece— Sicily, where Aeschylus died, and Macedon, where Euripides lived out his final years foremost among them—does not seem to have led to Athens losing its supremacy as the theatrical capital of the rapidly expanding world. Athens, and not only for the Athenians, was still at the center. Menander reputedly turned down unprecedented inducements to take his talents to Egypt.

What the Hellenistic period really marked was the rise in the status of the actor. The organization of a burgeoning acting profession took professionals all over the Greek world with a repertoire that could not survive on parochial appeal. Touring is expensive, and the size of a traveling company allowed no room for the luxury of a chorus-leader, never mind an entire chorus. This further contributed to its integration into the whole play becoming marginalized, even in revival of the classic tragedies.

By the time of Menander, the function of the chorus has carried this tendency to its logical conclusion. *The Malcontent* and *The Woman from Samos* have a five-act structure. At the end of each act the characters exit. Time passes, enough to carry forward the action to the next point of dramatic interest. The audience take a breather: so do the actors. What then of the chorus who, as we have seen, were the wellspring of earlier drama but found a diminishing role among domestic concerns and the subtleties of individual interaction? This is how the four entr'actes in *The Malcontent* are indicated in the script:

End of Act One

DAOS: . . . I ought to let her brother know about this so we can arrange to keep an eye on the girl. In fact, I'd better do that right now. Look, here's a group of drunks heading for the shrine. I don't think I want to get involved with that lot.

(*Exit Daos*)

CHOROU   (227–32)

End of Act Two

GETAS: You're a good cook as cooks go, I've always said so, but I still wouldn't trust you further than I could toss you.

(*Exeunt Sikon and Getas*)

CHOROU   (425–26)

End of Act Three

GORGIAS: I really can't leave mother by herself. See to what she needs, Daos. I won't be long.

(*Exeunt severally Sostratos, Gorgias, and Daos*)

CHOROU   (617–19)

End of Act Four

SOSTRATOS: It won't take me long. I'll come and fetch you directly.

(*Exeunt severally Sostratos and Gorgias*)

CHOROU   (784)

The presence and loose identity of the chorus are announced the first time they appear, and, after that, they simply arrive to pass the time. The same seems to be true in *The Woman from Samos*, but the missing portion of manuscript at the end of the first act makes it impossible to know whether the chorus are introduced in a similar cavalier fashion. The end of the first acts of *The Arbitration* and *The Shorn Girl* suggest that it is a convention:

CHAIRESTRATOS: Let's be off. There's a crowd of drunks coming this way. We'd be best off avoiding them. (*The Arbitration* 169–71)

DAOS: There's a gang of lads on the way, drunk most of them. I do applaud the mistress. The girl can stay with us. That's a real mother for you. Now for the young master. Time for him to come home, I think. And the sooner the better. (*The Shorn Girl* 260–66)

The apparent reduction of the once noble centerpiece of the entire drama to an unmannerly rabble might seem the most horrendous of declines. If the chorus were really the reflection of the democratic spirit of Athens itself, then

Menander is merely a Platonic shadow of the true drama as it sinks into merited obscurity. The truth is that he does reflect a new era but arguably one that is every bit as interesting and dramatic as that which went before. Menander's relegation of the chorus extends one step further the inexorable advance of character over plot. He finds a new dimension for comedy, the individual voice that depends on no corporate onstage response. The chorus can do no more than provide *entr'actes* to break up dramatic scenes that already incorporate those moments of reflection which the chorus had traditionally supplied.

Aristophanes named many of his plays after the chorus, a chorus whose theatrical potential is barely reflected by the lines on a page. A major challenge to a modern director of *Clouds*, *Birds*, or *Frogs* is to create a play's mood through the chorus. It is no less true for *Acharnians*, *Lysistrata*, or *Festival Time* where the choruses represent humans, not anthropomorphic figures. The chorus are integral to the performance structure. The two late Aristophanes plays, *Women in Power* and *Wealth*, were from a time when the festivals had begun to alter in emphasis but still preserved the patriotic fiction of Athens as the only city that mattered.

Menander's plays offer no such conviction; hence the chorus have lost that positive role. It can be no more than conjecture to suggest how these interludes may have linked the scenes but they could have occupied some time and they could have had some acceptable theatrical function. The absence of a text deemed worth recording may indicate that they used no words. The plays as they stand do not look as though they would have been enhanced by the invasion of a set of drunken buffoons, but behind the single stage direction *chorou* could have been all the joy and fun of the chorus of operetta. In adapting Greek comedy, Plautus was to drop the chorus altogether and incorporate musical interludes into his plays. Whole sequences are thought to have been sung.[5] If that was so, then Menander could have offered an important transitional stage through which comedy traveled.

There are other possibilities. Some of Menander's comedy is of the knockabout kind typified by traditional characters such as cooks and running slaves who seldom pause to take breath, cooks because they are talking too much and slaves because they are trying to evade somebody who is after their blood. Elsewhere, the rhythm of a play is dictated by subtler response as believable people try to keep their feet in a world strewn with banana skins. Could the chorus have provided some kind of tonal link, pointing to the way in which the comic and the serious inhabit one another's worlds?

In *The Woman from Samos*, each act opens with a description of some off-stage action. Might a choral interlude have offered such action in dumbshow to prepare the audience for what came next? Or simply offer a breather, an opportunity to relax for an audience that could not afford to miss much within the main action?

The fifth-century world where the chorus were the dramatic contact point between audience and actor and where the individual had civic responsibilities on which his civil rights depended is long gone. This is Hellenistic Athens. Such a change of social focus is also a means of addressing the paradox of the physical conditions under which Menander's plays were performed. Put simply, this paradox relates to the fact that the domestic trend in drama as represented by New Comedy coincides with the building of the first stone theatre in Athens, a permanent building constructed by Lykurgus on the site of a theatre whose temporary nature had been one of its virtues.

Lykurgus' theatre was effectively Europe's first playhouse. At least a hundred years too late it was to provide a venue for Europe's first plays by Europe's first playwrights which were put on in playing-spaces that had either been planned for other purposes or designed to be temporary and mobile. If this underestimates the planning that went into the Periklean stage of development in the precinct of Dionysus in the fifth century, there is little argument that that stage building had all the virtues of being both flexible and impermanent.

In Athens there had been a need for a theatrical space before there was a need for a theatre. Tragedy was introduced in the sixth century B.C. into the festival which was later to become the Great Dionysia. Displays and dance and epic recitation were performed in competition for thirty to forty years before the first indications of drama as an independent art form.

The Great Dionysia was only one of a number of occasions of civic importance where the community celebrated its own existence and its own survival. In honor of the god Dionysus, the Great Dionysia was a spring festival, held to coincide as far as possible with the resumption of the trading season when the Aegean again became navigable. Through Athenian history and on until the Christian era, the Great Dionysia continued to be the most public occasion for the presentation of plays in competition. The other dramatic festival of note was the Lenaia, held in December/January and hence more of a local than an international affair.

The earliest venue for the Great Dionysia was in the marketplace area, the Agora, where a temporary auditorium was built. All that has survived of this is a garbled story about a collapse of scaffolding at the performance of an early play of Aeschylus, round about the turn of the century from sixth to fifth. Tragedy then moved to the Precinct of Dionysus below the Acropolis. It was now some thirty years since the shadowy figure of Thespis had become the first playwright by creating dramatic text for performance by a single actor and a chorus.

The southeastern slope of the Acropolis provided a natural auditorium of sufficient size to accommodate large audiences. The Theatre of Dionysus is still there, tucked in below the Parthenon, though today it is no more than an archaeological site. What the site cannot tell us is what the theatre was actually like for the performance of any play of the time, tragic, satyric, or comic. Before Menander began to write, the theatre underwent substantial physical modifications, but we cannot be sure what it was like for his plays either. The reason is simple enough. In Roman times the whole theatre space was revamped along the lines of the adjacent Theatre of Herodes Atticus (second century A.D.), and those are the visible remains.

The generally accepted view is that the first theatre in the Precinct, the one for which Aeschylus wrote, was fairly rudimentary. In the middle of the fifth century B.C. Perikles included modernization and extension of the Precinct as part of his grand building plan which included the building of the Parthenon and the various smaller temples which adorn the Acropolis. This Periklean Theatre was still in its essence temporary, not, perhaps, in its basic organization of space, but in its stage building (*skene*) and the boundaries imposed on the playing area. In other words, however elaborate or simple, however formal or flexible, the scenic backing for the first performances of the majority of the classical repertoire could be removed. As in Burbage's Theater, there was little about the stage and its surrounds which could not be uprooted or transformed in an afternoon by a competent group of carpenters or stage crew.

The basic relationship between auditorium and performance space in the time of Perikles presumably harked back to the predramatic form of dance and music, the dithyramb, which was one of the influences, Aristotle believed, on early tragedy. The centerpiece was the *orchestra*, literally "dancing-place." This was the home of the chorus and was to remain so as long as the chorus were a feature of the drama. Most, though not all, commentators believe that it was circular with a diameter at various times of between 64 and 90 feet,[6] large enough, certainly, to serve for elaborate choric movement. To the north of the *orchestra* was the *theatron*, the audience space. Tiers of seats rose on a steep rake from the edge of the *orchestra* and over halfway round its circumference, back in fan shape and up the hillside. Though unlikely to have had as many rows as Argos with its eighty carved

from the rockface, a conservative estimate places the potential audience of
the Periklean Theatre at seventeen thousand. Plato's figure was as high as
thirty thousand. Here a substantial proportion of the citizen population
could be accommodated, as well as resident aliens and visitors to the city.
There is no good reason to suppose that women were excluded, particularly
those of the *hetaira* class, who did not yet feature as characters within the
plays but whose education and independence were greater than those
afforded to citizen women. The best seats were reserved for judges, priests,
and officials. Division of the auditorium into wedges reduced the problem
of allocating tickets and policing the house. The overall shape of the
theatron ensured that the whole audience saw the chorus patterned against
the background and physically located between themselves and the principal actors.

The actors' place was on the far side of the *orchestra*. Loosely described
as the stage, it was, in the Periklean Theatre, at most a wide but shallow
platform in front of the *skene*. The dimensions, even the existence, of such
a platform, are matters of dispute. In the absence of any remains, the most
plausible arguments are those that look directly at the requirements of the
plays which experienced playwrights were fashioning in full knowledge of
the available resources.[7]

Questions of scenery and stage machinery are no less bedeviled by a
conflict of approach. Some fifth-century plays require no more than a single
entrance into a palace background. Others call for a rural location
(Euripides' *Cyclops* and *Elektra*) or changes (as in Sophocles' *Ajax* from
before the protagonist's tent to the seashore), during the course of the action.
Aristophanes has characters gallivanting off to heaven and hell or building
a city in midair with all the abandon of a writer confident that his audience
will accompany him on any flight of the imagination he requires.

All personal preferences apart, there is at least common ground in
proposing that a theatre constructed of wood is potentially more flexible
than one constructed of stone. In scenic terms, the Theatre of Perikles must
have been a more versatile unit than the Theatre of Lykurgus which in the
time of Menander superseded it.

This makes it all the harder to account for that next stage in the theatre's
physical development, a development that is rather more easily traced
because it involved creating a permanent theatre. More than fifty years after
the death of Aristophanes, Lykurgus became treasurer of the Financial
Administration in Athens. His enthusiasm in this role seems to have been
fostered by a mission to recreate the Athens of Perikles. Over a hundred

years after Perikles' creation of the theatre that bore his name Lykurgus fossilized it by making the stage-building and its surrounds out of stone.

The curiosity in this matter to the theatre historian is that Lykurgus' enforcement of a solidity on the theatre structure coincides with the movement toward small-town realism of which Menander was the prime exponent. Menander's first play was presented less than ten years after the building of the Lykurgan edifice. Much of this book is concerned with pointing out Menander's realism. The question can no longer be ducked as to how effective or even intelligible such realism might have been, presented in stage conditions more appropriate to Wagnerian opera.

If any answer is to be found, it is likely to relate to a number of features of stage performance and the way in which Menander's theatre, no less than that of Euripides or Aristophanes, or Shakespeare or Molière if it comes to that, wrote within a frame of reference bounded by audience expectation. If the trademark of all those playwrights was the capacity to take the spectator by surprise, there was always a root tradition. Theatre has always been a matter of convention, but convention implies common ground, a contract or agreement to do things in a certain kind of way. The Greeks had their innovators, Euripides and Menander among them, but there was no medium for an avant-garde. Euripides made the most headway in the advance toward realism by "filling his stage with cripples and beggars" as the fictional Aeschylus puts it in Aristophanes' *Frogs*. Yet his "realistic" beggars wore masks and worked within an emblematic tradition that had made no more than a single concession to realism. A modern audience familiar from birth with the literalness of film and television will find it hard to envisage the shock felt by a fifth-century B.C. audience confronted in a tragedy with the merest token of life as it was really lived. Perhaps the nearest equivalent was the outcry among traditional classicists when the classical playwrights began to make their stage comeback costumed by the imaginations of contemporary directors.

To take the argument further requires a closer consideration of precisely how the comedies of Menander may have been staged and acted. The Lykurgan Theatre provided a stone edifice, probably of two storeys. The stage at some time was raised to between 10 and 12 feet in height. This is confirmed by the Roman architect Vitruvius who compares what he describes simply as "the Greek stage" with the lower, 5-foot stage, of the standard Roman theatre.[8] Such a high stage seems impractical in the Periklean Theatre when all the surviving playwrights appear to write scenes in which there is easy, if irregular, access between stage and *orchestra*.

From the middle of the fourth century onward, theatre building became a feature of town planning in any community that took itself seriously. For the most part these theatres, many of which survive in a better state of preservation than are those in the main centers, do support the idea of a high stage. Vitruvius was, after all, an architect. He was unlikely to get his measurements wrong even if his history was vague. "The Greek theatre" could, of course, refer to anything from the time of Aeschylus to theatres in Greece in his own time—he wrote *On Architecture* shortly before the birth of Christ. One of the central differences between the theatre of the classical period and that of Menander, as we have already seen, was the change in the importance of the chorus as an integrated element within the play. However memorable or rhythmically significant in the total performance, the chorus in a Menander play could comfortably perform in a reserved area 10 feet below the main action without in any way diminishing the impact of the play as a whole.

As far as settings are concerned, the plays and fragments that we have suggest that Menander was content to rely on the simplest of stage effects. *The Malcontent* prologue sets the scene:

PAN: We are in Attica. Suppose it so for now.
    The village of Phyle and for all Phylesians,
    This shrine from which I entered is sacred to the Nymphs.
    The locals farm this stony waste somehow, and it's a holy place.
    Here to my right, your left, lives Knemon . . . (1–5)

Nothing here suggests that the playwright has any interest in setting his scene in any way other than by words. "Suppose it so for now," literally "Imagine it," has a similar force to Plautus' introduction to the scene in *Menaechmi*:

All this is Epidamnus. As long as this play lasts anyway.
Another play, another place. (Plautus, *Menaechmi*, 72–74)

For *The Malcontent*, stage right is Knemon's house, and stage left, as we soon discover, that of his estranged wife and stepson. These houses may well have been signaled by a portico, not to imply the status of the owners—both families are living hand to mouth—but in order to distinguish them from Pan's shrine which separates them. All that the setting requires is the three entrances, Knemon's house, perhaps, to include the familiar wheeled platform known as the *ekkuklema*.

The Woman from Samos does not even have recourse to the central entrance, requiring only the adjacent houses of Demeas and Nikeratos. Other plays seem equally predictable: a street in Athens (*The Arbitration, The Shield, The Man She Hated, The Farmer,* and *The Harpist*); in Corinth (*The Shorn Girl*); in Eleusis (*The Sikyonian*). None appears to need more than two houses, though, as with *The Malcontent,* two additional exits are required, to town and country. David Wiles identifies the significance of this: "It is to be noted that Menander's theatre operates on a horizontal plane, and makes no use of height. . . . In Menander, love is not a spiritual but an earthly affair."[9]

This rejection of the intricacies of staging is one way in which Menander focuses his world and narrows it. The theatre may be an enormous one with an audience of many thousand, but the action is confined. The characters have few places to hide and little room to maneuver. In spatial terms the sense of performance cannot but bring to mind the marionette theatre. The puppet is and always has been as capable of presenting the domestic situation as the heroic or farcical: so was it to prove, in the hands of Menander, with the Athenian theatre, despite the remoteness of its audience and the unreality of its masked players. In Menander's theatre the major issues of state became subordinate to those of daily living. The construction of the theatre which abandoned the *orchestra* as a meeting place of audience and performer offered instead a direct contact. Direct address between actor and audience had been a feature of the comedy of Aristophanes, but Menander heralds a new intimacy. In *The Woman from Samos* the centering of the play on Demeas and his adopted son Moschion is reinforced by both of them sharing their feelings with the audience, addressing them, indeed, as *andres,* "gentlemen." The comic potential of the device revolves around the audience's superior knowledge of what has really happened but with no means of apprising those on stage.

These solo scenes require a kind of playing that is abetted by the actors' wearing of masks. Until recent years, the technique of masked acting was so little understood by those who wrote about Greek performance that the mask was treated as a restriction on the actor's mobility, a handicap that the actor must overcome in order to get across to the audience the rudiments of personality. This reading of Greek performance is all the more distressing for having been compounded by some of those who sought to create authenticity by using masks in the revival of Greek comedies and tragedies without treating the mask as the central feature of a performing style. Acting in masks, we were meant to believe, was something that actors grew out of when they became subtle enough not to need them and the theatres grew intimate enough for the mask to become redundant. The implication of this is that a playwright such as Menander would have done away with the mask had the size of his theatre and the expectations of his audience made such a thing possible. There is no evidence of any kind, in his plays or anywhere else, to suggest that this is a view based on anything other than prejudice.

On one notable occasion, Menander does make use of the mask for the sake of a stage gag. In *The Malcontent* the young man Sostratos is persuaded to go and do a day's digging in Gorgias' fields in order to impress Knemon with his industry. Knemon never turns up. When Sostratos returns in Act Three, he complains to the audience about how exhausted he is by his efforts under a baking sun. The next character to enter is his slave Getas:

SOSTRATOS: Hey Getas.

GETAS: Who wants me?

SOSTRATOS: I do.

GETAS: Who are you, then?

SOSTRATOS: Are you blind?

GETAS: Oh, Master. It's you. (*The Malcontent* 551–53)

The point behind the exchange only becomes clear when Gorgias introduces Knemon to Sostratos who greets him with the words: "Quite a tan. Farmer, is he?" (756). Sostratos, it is quite clear, makes his second entrance wearing a different mask, a dark one to show how much he has caught the sun.

For the most part, the mask is not used for the trick effect; it is used, at least in part, to identify character. The grammarian Julius Pollux, writing in the second century A.D. provided a catalogue of forty-four types of mask.[10] These are divided into groups: old men; young men; slaves; women; and specialist masks. He adds, however, that portrait masks, as in Old Comedy, were made as close as possible to the original. This list has been the source of a number of studies in the present century, many of which seek to identify masks from the list with pictorial representation of masked actors to be found on monuments or vase-paintings: or with the various characters in the surviving plays and fragments of New Comedy.[11]

David Wiles's invaluable recent study[12] points to the limitations of most of these studies. In the first place, there is no supporting evidence that Pollux's list is, or was, comprehensive. More importantly, the mask had tended to be seen, as noted above, as a limiting factor on the playwright and the range of his characters. Wiles treats the mask "not as a naturalistic portrait, but as a system of signs." He proceeds to draw the sophisticated theatrical conclusion that in performance spectators perceived the masks less as a set of masks in themselves than as a succession of transformations: "We need to understand the spectator's perception as a process" (p. 83). Such a conclusion fits perfectly with the "sunburn" joke. More broadly, it frees Menander from the limitations imposed by the term "stock character" without attributing to the Athenian playgoer an unwarranted intellectualism.

There were restrictions on the range of characters in the plays and the range of their activities. These restrictions were in part the product of a society that limited the roles of individuals. The grouping of characters by status, gender, and profession was inevitable because society was geared to upholding such barriers. *The Malcontent* has a cast of two poor farmers, one rich farmer and his son, four slaves, two professionals (cook and parasite), and two women. *The Woman from Samos* has one poor man, one rich man and his son, one slave, and two professionals (cook and courtesan). This, of course, is only part of the story. To insist on formulae is to deny the variety of contrasts and changes of status that give Menander his immense dramatic versatility.

Masked playing emphasizes some aspects of nonmasked comic technique, the way in which the actor will handle the double take, the misunderstanding, the driving of a scene. What are these but physical reactions, a rapid move of the head, a turn away, a lift of the chin, a shrug? Menander's comedy is carried by the pace of entrances and exits. Characters' moods are signposted by the way in which they walk. Acting in a mask draws attention to the feet as much as to the head because posture and stance give the messages of the eyes in film or television.

The mask tends in the theatre to overshadow other aspects of costume, but here in Menander's plays it seems likely that convention with regard to costume combined the artifice of an emblematic tradition with social costume that would echo that of real life. In the comedies of Aristophanes, many male characters had sported the phallus, strapped on over tights and with a short tunic to emphasize its presence. Though many of the comic vase-paintings of the fourth and third centuries show dramatic scenes of characters who do wear a phallus, these are for the most part mythological burlesques and a far cry from Menander's world. A far better guide is offered by a series of mosaics (see illustrations 9, 10, 11, and 12) that simply show conventional everyday costume for main characters with some recognizable features for those with specific attributes.

Such comparative realism is supported by Pollux in the *Onomasticon* and backed, though not in its detail, by Donatus' *On Comedy*.[13] They refer to specific color coding—yellow for courtesans, purple for young men, and so on—and identifying props or mannerisms—a twisted cloak for a parasite, a hooked stick for an old man.[14] The various mask-types, as Wiles shows, necessarily accorded with variations in costume, complementing them and serving as a kind of visual shorthand for the audience.

The dramatic device that gives *The Woman from Samos* its comic impetus is the regular one of having two characters out of harmony with one another's reading of events: a prototype mask situation. Act One opens with Moschion in a state of anxiety over his father's return. He eventually leaves the stage wondering if he would be best off going to hang himself. Demeas, his father, enters immediately, delighted to be home but concerned about telling Moschion of the marriage he has arranged for him. He then goes into his house.

Act Two opens with Demeas emerging in a rage after finding a baby there. His encounter with Moschion begins with Moschion full of concern and ends with him leaving, everything apparently resolved. Demeas eventually returns to his house at the end of the act equally satisfied that everything is working out right.

Act Three has a new reversal with Demeas returning in a greater turmoil than ever after coming to the mistaken conclusion that Moschion has fathered a child on the woman his father is living with. And so the complications are compounded through Act Four until the point of resolution, which is delayed by Menander to introduce an additional surprise into the final act. The dramatic shape makes use of a theatrical means. This is not to suggest that a play of Menander could not be adequately performed except by masked actors. It is to show that the physical demands of the masked performance in a theatre of huge dimension are not out of keeping with the subtle nuances of the domestic situation and the emotions of affection as well as of passion.

Vase-paintings from various periods have been used as evidence of the way in which scenes in Greek tragedy or comedy were staged.[15] Welcome as such illustrations may be in the absence of any other visual information, they have to be viewed with care even when they appear to advertise their association with the theatre by showing an actual platform stage, or actors in costume. Many of the proposed "theatrical scenes" could as easily be an illustration from a poem or simple decoration based on a familiar story. Those that clearly identify a stage or actors all too seldom relate to any of the pitifully small number of plays we possess from the classic repertoire.

In comparatively recent times, a series of mosaics have been unearthed in Mytilene whose inspiration in plays of Menander brooks no argument.[16] Not only are characters identified by name but plays are given by title. These mosaics are dated several hundred years after the first performance of Menander originals, but they closely resemble two other mosaics of Diosk-ourides based on originals from Menander's time and do appear to give some indications of how specific scenes may have been staged. They also accord well with the mass of terracotta masks from the ancient world, including those from Lipari which are dated to, at most, within a generation of Menander's death. Comic scenes and stone reliefs from Delos, Ephesus, Pompeii, and elsewhere suggest a greater performance continuity than previously assumed. They demonstrate the stage and its background, in some cases scenery and machinery: more significantly, they give fine illustrations of the composition of scenes which involve actors in masks.

The Mytilene mosaics are of particular interest in that they identify scenes from known Menander plays, *Epitrepontes* (*The Arbitration*), *Mi-soumenos* (*The Man She Hated*), *Plokion* (*The Necklace*), and *Phasma* (*The Ghost*) among them. One scene labeled *Samias* (*The Woman from Samos*) was used to illustrate the Penguin Classics edition of Menander.[17] This shows a "still" from the scene in which Demeas rejects Chrysis and expels her from his home. The play and the three characters are all identified by name. Whether or not the mosaic reflects the manner of the first perform-ance of *The Woman from Samos*, it is an informative guide to the staging of the scene as it is written.

The Woman from Samos is a play of misunderstandings revolving around the parentage of the baby born during the absence of Demeas and his neighbor Nikeratos on business. Demeas has forbidden Chrysis, the Samian woman with whom he lives, to have a child. Demeas' adopted son, Moschion, has seduced Nikeratos' daughter, and she has given birth to a baby. Everyone is frightened to admit the truth even when Demeas discovers that there is a baby in his house. Act Three opens with the entrance of Demeas after overhearing the old Nurse refer to the baby as being the son of Moschion and subsequently catching sight of his Samian breastfeeding the baby. His reaction is to assume that Chrysis is the mother and that she must have seduced Moschion. The entry of the slave Parmenon compounds the misunderstanding when Demeas tells him he knows the truth while declining to say what he means. Demeas' "truth" is not the same as Parmenon's. The next scene has Demeas throwing Chrysis out of his house, but the savagery with which he does so is set against the chance presence of the Cook. Although he has no idea what is going on, the Cook's interruptions offer a comic counterpoint to Demeas' shocking denunciation of Chrysis as a common whore. Part of the dialogue runs as follows:

CHRYSIS: This is terrible.

DEMEAS: Terrible, yes. Tears too? Tragic. I'll soon stop you . . .

CHRYSIS: Stop me what?

DEMEAS: Nothing. You've got the child, you've got the old woman. Now, clear off.

CHRYSIS: All because I kept the baby?

DEMEAS: Amongst other things.

CHRYSIS: What other things?

DEMEAS: Because of that.

COOK: So that's what all the excitement's about?

CHRYSIS: I don't understand.

DEMEAS: You didn't appreciate when you were well off, did you?

CHRYSIS: Didn't appreciate? What are you talking about?

DEMEAS: You came to this house with the clothes you stood up in. You know what I'm talking about. One thin frock.

CHRYSIS: So?

DEMEAS: I was everything to you. You were nothing.

CHRYSIS: Who's nothing now?

DEMEAS: Don't bandy words with me, Chrysis. You have your own things. You can keep the slaves and the jewellery. Now, out of my house.

COOK: It's a very angry man we've got here. I'll have a word. Excuse me, sir . . .

DEMEAS: Are you addressing me?

COOK: Don't bite.

DEMEAS: Any girl would jump at what I can offer and thank god for it.

COOK: What's he on about?

DEMEAS: You've got a son. You have everything.[18]

COOK: Not been bitten yet. Try again. All the same . . .

DEMEAS: If you say another word to me, I'll punch your head in.

COOK: Quite right. Absolutely. Well, then. I'll be back off indoors.

Exit Cook

DEMEAS: Something special, are you? You'll soon find out how you rate in the city. Ten drachmas a go and a free dinner. Till you die of drink. If you don't like the idea of that, then starve. You'll learn. Nobody quicker. And you'll realise what a mistake you made. Just keep out of my way. (369–98)

This is as revealing a scene as any in Menander, both for the social assumptions on which it is based and for the manner in which the playwright has inserted such a vicious scene into what is meant to be a comedy. Demeas is legally in the right. Chrysis is in his house by invitation. Whatever her birth or status as a free woman, she has no legal entitlement to a stable relationship. She lives in Demeas' house for as long as he is prepared to tolerate her. The alternative is to look after herself, and the only way she can do that is by being a common prostitute.

The Mytilene mosaic offers further details on the staging and playing of the scene. Chrysis is to the viewer's right, her feet turned away from Demeas with the weight on the left leg. Her right arm is raised, and she is playing off the right shoulder, with her head turned in toward Demeas. Her pose is reminiscent of the famous Rieti statuette of a Roman tragic actor, for so long mistakenly taken as evidence of the *cothurnus* being a high-soled boot. Chrysis has an elaborate dress and a jewelled headdress, but her pose is that of a tragic figure.[19]

In the center is Demeas. He is leaning forward, his weight firmly on the left leg and with his right arm raised, fingers outstretched to within inches of Chrysis' face. He is portrayed as an old man. His mask is dark, his hair white, and in his left hand he carries a stick. Middle age does not seem to exist in Menander. The characters are either young or old which makes, perhaps, for more blatant conflict between generations. Although Demeas' age pushes him more toward a comic than a serious figure, his emotions are powerful enough and the physical relationship between Demeas and Chrysis is sufficiently compelling for the scene to play as uncompromisingly as it reads.

The only disarming factor is the presence of a witness, the Cook, pictured as dark-skinned, perhaps an African, with dreadlocks. Stationed at Demeas' shoulder, he is physically closer to him than Demeas is to Chrysis. His relaxed posture and look of engaged disinterest effectively distance him, and save the audience from being overwhelmed by a rejection so callous it would be difficult to imagine the relationship of Demeas and Chrysis ever recovering. It is still an uncomfortable scene. Here, surely, is the true explanation for Menander's reputation as a realistic playwright working within a tradition of large-scale artifice. When his characters let loose at one another, they pull no punches. What happens to Chrysis is what could happen in real life to any woman of the time dependent on a man in Demeas' position.

The interruption by the Cook in *The Woman from Samos* shows the serious penetrated by the absurd, a pattern used extensively elsewhere in the play. Another potentially vicious scene occurs in *The Malcontent* with the persecution of the misanthropic Knemon by another cook, Sikon, together with Sostratos' slave Getas. The disarming device here is a musical accompaniment as the final scene gradually turns into a finale. After line 879, the manuscript includes one of the few stage directions apart from *chorou* to be found in ancient texts, *aulei*, "the piper plays." The verse changes from iambic trimeters to tetrameters, and the burlesque sequence of hauling the old man from his house and banging on his door gives way to a curiously high-flown and extravagant passage from Sikon:

> These women in your life
> Met with warmth and affection.
> Your wife and your daughter
> Charmed all they encountered.
> Besides there was food, a wonderful spread,
> And convivial drinking for everyone present.
> Still listening? Don't fall asleep on me. (*The Malcontent* 936–41)

Eventually, Knemon is persuaded from his sickbed into a dance with which the play is wrapped up. Everything here suggests an extended musical sequence that, beyond the play proper, allows Knemon to be rehabilitated as a member of the wedding party. It is an ending more Hollywood than Molière, but it does not detract too greatly from the play's toughness elsewhere. Much would have depended on the manner of the playing of Knemon, a character some of whose complaints against the world must have struck a chord of sympathy, as do those of Alceste or Malvolio in Molière's *The Misanthrope* and Shakespeare's *Twelfth Night*.

The art of acting in a mask, whether in tragedy or comedy, would have been handed down from generation to generation, only in part influenced by the changing nature of the plays. Quintilian, the Roman rhetorician, has an interesting comparison between two comic stars of a different age, one of whom "has unique gifts in hand gesture," and the other "great nimbleness on his feet and speed of movement." He compares their voices too and their methods of handling an audience, concluding that "if either had tried the tricks of the other, it would have looked dreadful."[20] We do not know with what repertoire these two actors had enchanted Quintilian who lived in Rome in the first century A.D. It is clear, though, that by his time, the comic actor was recognizable on stage despite his mask and specialized in a certain range of role. It is interesting to speculate whether the same might have been true for the actor at the time of Menander. It also raises the question of doubling.

Dividing the number of roles among three actors[21] presents few problems in tragedy of the fifth century B.C. as long as it can be accepted that an actor did not specialize in, for example, female roles or gods. The only major difficulty occurs with reference to Sophocles' posthumously performed *Oedipus at Colonus* which either needs four actors to play it or to have Theseus played by each actor on different occasions. The problem is greater in Old Comedy with several of the plays of Aristophanes, notably *Lysistrata* and *Frogs*, including scenes with more than three speaking characters present. Financial as much as artistic considerations seem to have been responsible for the limited number of actors used in fifth-century tragedy, with the state paying for three actors per group submission and the *choregos* meeting any additional expenses.

Not enough is known about theatre organization in Athens in the latter part of the fourth century[22] to say whether any such financial reason would have imposed a limit on Menander, but it has been generally assumed that he did write for a company of three.[23] This remains the orthodoxy, unchallenged, as far as I know, by anyone including Wiles. K. B. Frost, to give him his due, necessarily considers the question in some detail.[24] Frost points out that no surviving scene has more than three speakers; that some characters fail to speak when they might be expected to; and that some characters appear to make an early exit to prepare the way for a new arrival. Now it may well be that Menander did write exclusively, for whatever reason, three-hander scenes, but the theatrical implications of a restriction on actors cannot simply be ignored. Not only is the possibility of Quintilian's individual acting talents submerged in apparently interchangeable performance styles, but, as Frost does confess, "A necessary consequence of recognising a three-actor rule is the acceptance of part-splitting, whereby a character is played by more than one speaking actor in the course of the play."

Of the two plays that are now almost complete, *The Woman from Samos* would appear the easier to resolve. There are six speaking roles, Demeas and Nikeratos (the two old men), Moschion (Demeas' son), Parmenon (the slave), Chrysis (the Samian), and the Cook who has no name. Demeas and Nikeratos appear in all five acts; Moschion, Chrysis, and Parmenon in four; the Cook in Act Three only and never at the same time as Nikeratos, himself the smallest of the major roles.

Demeas, Chrysis, and Parmenon all appear in a scene with the other characters. Though hardly an argument in itself, this looks remarkably like a playwright writing for a company of five. If the roles are to be split among three actors, it appears inevitable that one actor will play Moschion in Acts One, Two, Four, and Five; also, Parmenon and Chrysis in Act Three; also Chrysis as well as Moschion in Act Four.

A second actor will play Demeas in all five acts; also Chrysis in Act One; Parmenon in Act Two; and Nikeratos in Act Five.

The third actor will play Nikeratos in Acts One, Two, Three, and Four, but not in Act Five; also Parmenon in Act One; the Cook in Act Three; and Parmenon rather than Nikeratos in Act Five in which, anyway, Chrysis does appear but does not speak. Such an arrangement is technically possible but surely demands some powerful imperative.

The Malcontent, with a cast of three, becomes an absolute nightmare for the actors. Possible combinations are too complex to rehearse here, but with at least thirteen characters, perhaps as many as seventeen, the players would need to be superhuman. This, for example, is the pattern of action in the 170 lines of Act Four.

Enter Simiche

Enter Sikon

Enter Gorgias

Enter Sostratos (nonspeaking)

Exeunt Gorgias, Simiche, and Sostratos

Exit Sikon

Enter Sostratos (speaking)

Enter Gorgias and Knemon

Exit Gorgias

Enter Gorgias and Myrrhine (possibly nonspeaking—the text is deficient)

Exeunt Knemon and Myrrhine

Enter Kallippides

Exit Kallippides

Exeunt Sostratos and Gorgias

Sostratos, the only character to appear in all five acts, confuses the issue rather than clarifying it; such is the multiplicity of character combinations afforded within each act, never mind in the whole play. Sostratos, Knemon, and Gorgias each encounter nine other characters at one time or another. Six others meet at least four. The smallest number of actors required to tackle the play, allowing for doubling but not cross-casting, is, I believe, six. When every other salient feature of stage production at the time points to theatrical common sense on behalf of playwrights and those in charge of production, it will take more than circumstantial evidence to convince me that the Menander cast was restricted to three.

The final question to ask, if not answer, is how far the world of Menander that his plays propose is a truthful reflection of life in Athens in the final years of the fourth century B.C. Clearly, the stage, and especially the comic stage, is a place creating a special world. The history of stage revival was for many years overburdened with the problem of creating the "style" of classic plays. The production of a Restoration Comedy was an exercise in creating the clothes and accessories of the times of Charles the Second in order to recreate the late seventeenth century. From Charles Kean in the British theatre until at least the 1960s, antiquarianism was a means of giving the stage authenticity. It was as though the resurrection of a lost play was to be given marks out of ten according to how close it came to recreating, not the first ever production, but the actual era in which the play was written.

The virtue in so doing was exploded by those directors who perceived that the great plays of any period reflect only in part the time in which they were written, and then obliquely. The other part of the playwright's art consists in building from scratch a scene which belongs simultaneously to no period that has ever been and to every stage world there ever was. Such was Shakepeare's Venice, Troy, or Illyria as much as are Brecht's Padua, Chicago, or Setzuan.

The Athens of the late fifth century is better brought to life in the plays of Aristophanes than in the history of Thucydides or the dialogues of Plato. The concerns of ordinary citizens and the processes of their everyday lives emerge not from any naturalistic portrayal of character, location, or situation, but from a curious world of gods, heroes, and real people in a fictional guise mixed in with fictional people in a real guise. How do we know that they are the representatives of the real Athens rather than figments as rare as the creatures encountered by Odysseus on his prolonged return home from Troy? We cannot know for sure, but the combination of detail and the range of mundane activity in and among the fantasy smells right and feels right. We may reject Aristophanes' portrait of Sokrates swinging in his balloon or Euripides wheeled on stage in his study, but what are these characters but images of the popular notion of the intellectual based on all the prejudice and narrow-mindedness of the audience for whom he was writing? Between the lines of an Aristophanes play, whether set in the midair Cloudcuckooland or the subterranean abode of Pluto, is Athens itself, war-torn, anxious, and heading for disaster.

Menander's Athens was a quieter place, though hardly as quiet as his plays suggest. The stage world he presents is one where the principal preoccupations of the characters are making a living and making love. For the poor life is hard; for slaves life is unfair; for women life is limited; and for everyone life is unpredictable. The major difference from the world of Aristophanes is the lack of threat to Menander's characters from anything but one another. There may be wars off-stage, and the opening of *The Shield* offers good cause to exonerate Menander from charges of escapism, but government is stable or, if unstable, that is not the playwright's business.

At the same time, as Wiles has pointed out, Menander's theatre is ideological as is the theatre of Plautus, geared to a specific relationship with a specific audience. Plautus' world is wholly artificial because it is an amalgam of Menander's character and situation from the fourth century and his own stage practice and audience expectation from a hundred and fifty years later. Hence the sense in a Plautus play, and to a lesser extent in one of Terence, that the play brings everything to a conclusion. Menander's truth points to a world before the play opens and another after it finishes. Relationships grow, develop, and change. There is some point in speculating about the future of Knemon or of Chrysis because their life has been sufficiently rich and complex to be more than an excuse for a laugh or a parable on how to behave.

It is this capacity for creating people about whom it is possible to care that marks Menander, as we shall later see, as the founder of a European comic tradition that is based not on the belly-laugh—the history of that is as old as time—or on the artifice of high comedy or even comedy of manners, but rooted in sympathy: sympathy for those who are as much a part of the human condition as we are and who, in two thousand three hundred years, have changed remarkably little.

NOTES

1. It is wrong to assume that any playwright's characters, especially those of Euripides, represent his own views, but there is enough antiforeign sentiment expressed in plays such as *Andromache*, the *Bacchae*, and *Iphigeneia in Aulis* for it to appear common currency of the times.

2. J. B. Bury, *The Hellenistic Age*, Cambridge: Cambridge University Press, 1925, p. 26.

3. See M. Camp, *The Athenian Agora*, London: Thames and Hudson, 1986, pp. 46f.

4. At lines 729 and 876.

5. Michael Grant, delivering a lecture on Plautus in 1973, insisted on calling the *fabula palliata* (Roman comedy adapted from the Greek) "Roman opera."

6. The rectilinear shape of the theatre at Thoricos is well known. See E. R. Gebhard, *The Theatre at Isthmia*, Chicago: Chicago University Press, 1973, pp. 137–41, for a challenge to the circularity of the orchestra as the norm.

7. See both Arnott, *Public and Performance in the Greek Theatre*, London: Routledge, 1989 and Walton, *Greek Theatre Practice*, Westport, Conn.: Greenwood, 1980 and London: Methuen, 1991.

8. Vitruvius, *On Architecture*, Book V, 7.2 ff.

9. *The Masks of Menander: Sign and Meaning in Greek and Roman Performance*, Cambridge: Cambridge University Press, 1991, p. 65.

10. Julius Pollux, *Onomasticon*, IV 133–40.

11. See especially T.B.L. Webster, *Monuments Illustrating New Comedy*, London: London University Institute of Classical Studies, 1961. See also Mario Prosperi, "The Masks of Lipari," *The Drama Review*, 26, no. 4, 1982, pp. 25–36, on the use of the masks excavated at Lipari in a production of *The Woman from Samos*.

12. Wiles, *The Masks of Menander*, pp. 74–85 and passim.

13. Pollux, *Onomasticon*, IV 118–20: Donatus, *On Comedy*, VIII 6–7.

14. Translations of these texts and a comprehensive survey of questions relating to costume can be found in Wiles, *The Masks of Menander*, pp. 188–208.

15. See A. D. Trendall and T.B.L. Webster, *Illustrations of Greek Drama*, London: Phaidon, 1971.

16. A comprehensive assessment of these mosaics is to be found in S. L. Charitonides, L. Kahil, and R. Ginouvès, *Les Mosaiques de la Maison du Ménandre à Mytilène*, Bern: Antike Kunst, Sechstes Beiheft, 1970.

17. Translated by Norma Miller, London: Harmondsworth: Penguin, 1987.

18. A rehearsal improvement from the published text.

19. Lilly Kahil in an essay entitled *Remarques sur L'Iconographie des Pièces de Ménandre* in Fondation Hardt, Vol. 16, Vandoeuvres-Genève, 1969, assumes that Chrysis is carrying the baby, "un enfant emmaillote" (p. 238). This is by no means certain from the illustration, for it is not clear that her right arm is supporting anything and her left is by her side: nor is it necessarily suggested by Demeas' line "You've got the baby." Demeas adds, "you've got the old woman" who has no reason to be present (line 371). The scene establishes the baby's presence and in performance makes it a reference point for the action: so much so that in the Getty production the baby was also carried by Chrysis in Act One.

20. Quintilian XI, 3, 178ff.

21. For a review of the evidence, see Walton, *Greek Theatre Practice*, pp. 139–45.

22. The evidence from Guild records is comprehensively catalogued by G. M. Sifakis in *Studies in the History of Hellenistic Drama*, London: Athlone Press, 1967.

23. So F. H. Sandbach, "Menander and the Three-Actor Rule" in *Le Monde Grec: hommages a Claire Préaux*, Brussels: University of Brussels, 1975, pp. 197–204; also Wiles, *The Masks of Menander*. Kelley Rees in *The So-called Rule of Three Actors in the Classical Drama*, Chicago: University of Chicago Press,

1908, mounted a direct challenge to any notion of restricted numbers, but he was writing before the discovery of any complete plays of Menander.

24. *Exits and Entrances in Menander*, Oxford: Clarendon Press, 1988, pp. 2–5.

1. Menander and Theatrical Masks. Roman copy of Hellenistic original. (*The Art Museum, Princeton University. Museum purchase, Caroline G. Mather Fund. Bruce White Photography, Upper Montclair, NJ.*)

2. Portrait Bust of Menander. Roman herm, Artist unknown. Early first century A.D. Bronze. Height: 17 cm. Depth of base: 8-8.1 cm. *(Collection of the J. Paul Getty Museum, Malibu California.)*

3. New Comedy Scene. Marble relief believed to be of New Comedy scene. First century A.D. (*Museo Archeologico Nazionale, Naples.*)

4. Menander's "Theophoroumene." Mosaic by Dioscourides from second century B.C. *(Museo Archeologico Nazionale, Naples.)*

5. Group of Women from Unknown Play. Mosaic by Dioscourides from second century B.C. *(Museo Archeologico Nazionale, Naples.)*

6. Comic Actor (perhaps in the role of a parasite). Terracotta figure. Fourth century B.C. *(Reproduction by permission of the Syndics of the Fitzwilliam Museum, Cambridge.)*

7. Two Comic Masks. Greek terracotta. Date uncertain. *(Reproduction by permission of the Syndics of the Fitzwilliam Museum, Cambridge.)*

8. Two Comic Masks and Two Pipes. Roman mosaic. Second century A.D. *(Roma, Musei Capitolini. Reproduced by permission of Photographic Archive of the Musei Capitolini and Maria Teresa Natale.)*

Menander, "Samia." Mosaic. Third century A.D. *(Mytilene, House of Menander. The Department of Antiquities, Museum of Mytilene.)*

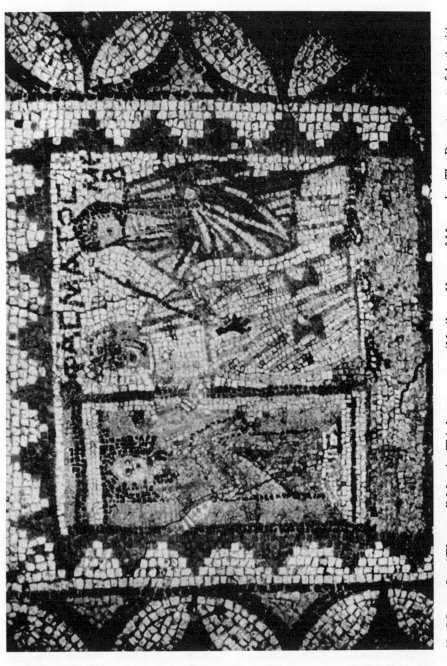

10. Menander, "Phasma." Mosaic. Third century A.D. (Mytilene, House of Menander. The Department of Antiquities,

11. Menander, "Epitrepontes." Mosaic. Third century A.D. *(Mytilene, House of Menander.
The Department of Antiquities, Museum of Mytilene.)*

12. **Menander, "Plokion."** Mosaic. Third century A.D. (Mytilene, House of Menander. The Department of Antiquities, Museum of Mytilene.)

Chapter 4

The Maker of Plays

There is a real sense in which Menander's work must have been formula-driven. His capacity to create was so prolific that, if the stories of his productivity are reliable, he would have experienced no difficulty working alongside Haydn with the Esterhazy family. It is precisely here, however, that enthusiasm for the reputation needs to be tempered by historical caution. There is rather better reason to believe that Haydn composed 104 symphonies than that Menander wrote 104 plays. To begin with, the symphonies survive and all of them are played, in all probability, in the course of any one year. Twenty productions of Menander in the last two thousand years is probably an optimistic estimate.

There are three main sources of the written works. First, there is the host of fragments, quotations, and references found in classical writings from the beginning of the third century B.C., when he died, on, into, and through the Roman period when his plays were known and appreciated by men of letters, if unstaged: where, too, his aphorisms were part of the literary currency. Augmenting these are references to Menander's works. Plutarch, a Boeotian Greek writing at the end of the first century A.D., provides the summary of a comparison between Aristophanes and Menander, which is informative about how a classical writer, though one with the advantage of three hundred years' critical hindsight, viewed the playwright's craft. He appears to point to Menander's ability to write differently for each character; to his charm and wit; and to his capacity to write for all members of an audience. Indeed, so enthusiastic is he that, not only is poor Aristophanes relegated to the reject pile, but so is everybody else:

> Why should any educated man ever go to the theatre, except to see a play of Menander's? . . . As painters, when their eyes are tired will look to the colours of flowers and grasses, so philosophers and literary men will turn to Menander as relief from their efforts, offering the mind the equivalent of flowery meadows and balmy breezes.[1]

Fascinating though such insights may be, they are a poor substitute for the real thing, and Plutarch offers here eight quotations from Aristophanes and not a single one from the Menander he adulates.

The second source for Menander is indirect and a minefield. Menander died around 290 B.C. Some hundred years later two playwrights writing in Latin—Plautus, a former actor, and Terence, a freed African slave—perfected the form of drama that was known at the time as the *fabula Palliata*. In Italy during the second century B.C., there was a variety of indigenous dramatic forms, history plays, native comedies, Roman tragedies, and local farces. Of these the *fabula Atellana*, with its fixed cast of four, may well be seen as a lynchpin of the "rough" theatre tradition whose full history is still to be written and which, by its very nature, may well never be.

In Rome the *fabula Palliata* was more popular than any other dramatic form. But it was popular because it was Greek: or rather because it was not Greek. Both Plautus and Terence paraded the fact that all their plays were based on the New Comedy of fourth- and third-century B.C. Athens. That meant Menander and any of another sixty playwrights whose names are known but whose plays are not. In effect, this comes down to Philemon and Diphilus writing before Menander, Apollodorus, and Demophilus contemporary to or after him. The plays were then adapted by Plautus and Terence and given a notably Roman flavor. Plots, characters, costume—*palliata* implies wearing Greek costume—setting, and moral tone were all Greek. This sounds as though it left little leeway for originality on the part of Plautus or Terence, but such a stricture would underestimate the extent of the adaptations—never mind the theatrical expectations of a Roman festival audience that boasted all manner of alternative distractions. The Latin language is skillfully exploited by both playwrights, and a musical element is introduced. The differences between Plautus and Terence are notable. Plautus is the marketplace technician, master of broad, boisterous farce where character is subordinate to situation. Here is a drive and energy that leaps from the page but is never quite at home there. So popular was Plautus with audiences that his name, never mind his plays, was pirated during his life and after his death as a guarantee of quality. We can trust the authenticity of the twenty-one surviving plays of Plautus—one incomplete—thanks to the energy of the grammarian Varro who took on the task of weeding out the poor attributions during the next century.

Terence started to write late as a result of his background as a slave, and he died young, apparently in a mishap at sea. All his six plays survive. The humor is gentler, and the characters are more subtle than those of Plautus. Ill-suited to the fairground conditions in which they had to be performed, the plays were not as successful with the public as those of Plautus had been. On the other hand, they appealed more to literary circles, both at the time and since. Terence, it would seem, owed more to Menander than did Plautus.

As it happens, we know from a variety of sources that both Plautus and Terence did adapt Menander plays. Plautus' *The Two Bacchises*, *The Casket* (*Cistellaria*), and *Stichus* are based on Menander originals: *Pseudolus*, *The Carthaginian* (*Poenulus*), and *The Pot of Gold* (*Aulularia*) may also be, the latter providing a number of parallels to Menander's *The Malcontent*. The details are complicated by the fact that, apart from a passage of about fifty lines from the middle of *The Two Bacchises*, no direct parallel survives from Menander with which to compare the Latin adaptation. Barely eighty lines of Menander's original, *The Double Deceiver*, have been recovered, but they do demonstrate both the debt owed by the Latin playwright and the original input for which he could take credit.

Of the six plays of Terence, no fewer than four are taken from Menander: *Brothers* (*Adelphi*), *The Girl from Andros* (*Andria*), *The Eunuch*, and *The Self-Tormentor* (*Heauton Timoroumenos*), which preserves its Greek title. Although there is no Menander original with which to make a direct comparison, the prologues of some of the Terence plays are as informative as any later critic could wish.

The Girl from Andros opens with a defense delivered by the speaker of the Prologue against attacks from rival playwrights, or, rather, one playwright, identified as Luscius Lanuvinus. Referring to himself in the third person—Terence was not himself an actor—he writes as follows:

This is my so-called error of judgement. Menander wrote two plays, *The Girl from Andros* and *The Girl from Perinthos*. If you know one, you know them both. The plots are more or less the same though there is a difference in language and treatment. Your playwright readily admits that he transferred certain suitable passages from Menander's *The Girl from Perinthos* to fit into his *Girl from Andros*. Now he is being pilloried for that, his enemies complaining that he ought not to "contaminate" one play with another. If that's a fault, then Naevius, Plautus and Ennius also stand accused. They started it and your playwright is following their example, a better one, he dare say, than the worthy pedantry of his detractors. (*The Girl from Andros* 9–21)

Other plays of Terence contain similar peevish prologues. *The Eunuch* begins by attacking Luscius Lanuvinus for ruining Menander's *Ghost* (*Phasma*) before revealing what happened at the first performance, or perhaps rehearsal, of *The Eunuch*, which, if true, offers some justification for his continued feud:

> What we are going to present is Menander's *The Eunuch*. The aediles bought it before but *he* got to see it. The official took his place. The play began. Then a shout from our friend. "He's a thief, not a playwright. He can't fool us. Naevius and Plautus both wrote a *Colax*. That's where he got his parasite from: and his boastful soldier." Well, if your playwright did make a mistake, it was an unwitting one. He's no plagiarist. Now you may be the judges. There is a *Colax* by Menander. That has a parasite called Colax and a boastful soldier. Our playwright is not trying to deny that he has transposed characters from the Greek into his play. What he does deny is that they had been used before in a Latin play. (*The Eunuch* 19–34)

The remainder of the Prologue is taken up with the impossibility of writing a play at all if one is not allowed to make use of stock characters. This playwright's confessional is as good evidence as we could wish that surviving Roman comedies are without exception based on Greek originals, and that seven, maybe as many as nine, are based on Menanders.

Sadly, this is not the same as saying that we have another seven plays of Menander, even in translation, to add to the meagre Greek texts. Terence is closer in mood to Menander than is Plautus, but he is still writing Roman plays, in Latin, for a Roman audience, more than a century after Menander's death. Only if the Menander originals were miraculously to make an unexpected entrance through the sands of Egypt, or via some uncharted library collection, might we be in a position to make an informed comparison between two creative artists, rather than between playwright and translator.

This leaves us with the third source of Menander, the plays themselves and actual fragments preserved in the various unlikely ways already described in Chapter 2. *The Malcontent* (*Duskolos*) is effectively complete. There are a few missing lines here and there, or incomplete beginnings and ends of lines where the manuscript is damaged. Nowhere is there a hiatus of the sort to make the sense unclear.

The same cannot be said for *The Woman from Samos* (*Samia*), for all I have been treating it as a complete play. The opening lines of the Prologue are lost, as is a further passage of some twenty to twenty-five lines later in the speech and as much again at the end before the entry of Chrysis, the Samian woman of the title. Her exit and that of the slave Parmenon are missing, as are the last fifteen or so lines of the first act.

When Act Two opens, after the choral interlude, Moschion is in the middle of a soliloquy, but his father Demeas appears to be already on stage. After brief greetings between father and son, two more passages of ten and about twenty-seven lines are lost or fragmentary, as is the very end of Act Two. From here on, a text is supplied from more than one source, and only a handful of individual lines are incomplete. The positive feature of this is that most of the missing one hundred and thirty or so lines are from the expositional scenes. The resolution is complete. So, effectively, is the plot which loses some refinements but can be supplied without too much creative input from the editor or translator. *The Woman from Samos* can, by the exercise of a little license, be claimed as a complete play.

Similar claims cannot be made for any of the other fragmentary plays, even though they contain longish passages of uninterrupted dialogue and, on occasion, whole acts. *The Arbitration* is the most complete but has lost most of Act One, a lot of Act Four, and all but two pages of Act Five. *The Shorn Girl* has an interesting prologue that turns out to be delayed, with the opening scene missing. Act Two is the most complete, but all the other acts lose over a hundred lines and some passages that are crucial for the sense. *The Shield* has a complete Act One but virtually no Four or Five. Of the remaining twelve plays identified by name in the Oxford Text,[2] only *The Farmer* (*Georgos*), *The Man She Hated* (*Misoumenos*) and *The Sikyonian* (*Sikuonios*) run to as many as a hundred lines.

Information can be gleaned from the smallest of these fragments. The danger, however, is to read too much into too little. I have recorded elsewhere the difficulties encountered earlier in the century by those who believed they could trace the plot of *The Woman from Samos* from the meagre information then available.[3] One of Menander's considerable skills as a playwright is his capacity to confound an audience's expectation. Few of these earlier critics got anywhere close to what we now know to be the plot line of a play whose twists and turns are legion. And who would have guessed, had four acts survived and the fifth alone gone missing, at the new direction that the play would take once the apparent difficulties of the characters have been overcome by the end of Act Four?

Much of the comprehensive and formidable work on Menander was undertaken by the late T.B.L. Webster. Immensely thorough and imaginatively, if not always theatrically aware, the problems of speculating on missing Menander are highlighted—indeed confessed—in the difference between the 1950 and the 1960 editions of his book *Studies in Menander*. The later edition contains an appendix on the *Duskolos* (*The Malcontent*) which first came to light between the two editions.[4]

The Malcontent opens with a Prologue from the God Pan in which he sets the scene and introduces the main characters and the plot. Sostratos, a wealthy young man, has fallen in love on sight with the daughter of Knemon, the malcontent, or bad-tempered man, of the play's title. Knemon was once married to a widow with a young son, Gorgias, from her previous marriage. She left Knemon, but they now live on either side of Pan's shrine. Sostratos makes the acquaintance of Gorgias who persuades him that Knemon may be impressed if he sees the young man working hard in Gorgias' fields alongside his own.

Knemon's plans to go and work in his fields are disrupted when Sostratos' mother arrives to organize a sacrifice at the shrine of Pan. Apart from the general disruption, there is a cook who wants to borrow implements, and Knemon decides he cannot leave his house unattended with so many strangers in the vicinity.

Simiche, his one and only servant, drops a bucket down the well. Trying to retrieve the bucket, Knemon falls down after it. A sunburned and exhausted Sostratos returns from the fields in time to give a notional hand in saving Knemon, who is actually rescued by his stepson Gorgias. A chastened, if not reformed, Knemon asks Gorgias to find a husband for his daughter, and plans are made for the wedding of the daughter to Sostratos. In a passage of what Webster aptly describes as "thug" comedy, the Cook and a slave take revenge on Knemon, and he is finally persuaded to attend the marriage feast.

In 1950 Webster had very little to go on and included a conjectural summary of this play alongside eight others known from fragment or reference elsewhere. "Pan speaks the formal prologue," wrote Webster. "Then, I suggest that, as in the *Aulularia* (of Plautus), a rich neighbour visits Knemon and arranges for his daughter to marry Knemon's son; the arrangements go foward in spite of Knemon's objection to any sort of festivity or geniality . . . and in spite of Knemon's son, who appeals to his father to use his money to help him marry the poor girl. Knemon is frightened and moves his gold to the shrine of Pan but it is discovered by a slave who makes off with it. Meanwhile the poor girl's mother appeals to her brother-in-law,

Knemon's rich neighbour . . . and, presumably, as in the *Aulularia*, the marriage is rearranged in favour of the poor girl."

No one would be so churlish as to condemn a scholar, particularly one of such formidable authority, for attempting to make an educated guess at what may have happened in a play from evidence that is at best flimsy: especially when that scholar was honest enough to include his summary in a new edition at a time when new information had proved him wrong. The fact remains that Webster was so wildly wide of the mark that it throws into disrepute a vast proportion of what he proposes elsewhere on equally gimcrack evidence.

This is a risk that is no longer worth taking. The fragmentary plays can offer insights into Menander's dramatic methods and his delineation of character. Too much attention paid to chance remarks or half-digested scenes is more likely, however, to lead to misinformation than to enlightenment. As it is, the one whole play, *The Malcontent*, and the one play, *The Woman from Samos*, which is almost complete do, between them, provide quite enough insight into how and why Menander's reputation should have become and remained so high in the Hellenistic and Roman worlds.

The structure of *The Malcontent* is more complex than the above plot summary implies. A Prologue from the God Pan sets the scene for the play and introduces the main character, cantankerous Knemon, who

> Never in his life volunteered a friendly word to anyone,
> Never made overtures to a living soul. (8–9)

The audience hears his past history:

> Nevertheless,
> A man like this got married once, to a widow,
> Recently bereaved and with a baby to support.
> He fought with her, day in, day out,
> And most of the night as well, like cat and dog.
> Somehow they had a daughter; which only made things worse.
> The relationship went sour to the point of no return.
> And she didn't. She left him, went to live with her son,
> The one from the previous marriage, who, as it happens,
> Lives here on the other side, eking out a living
> On the smallest of smallholdings. (14–24)

Pan's concern, however, is for Knemon's daughter, "an innocent, so protected there's not a mean thought in her head" (34). He has organized for a rich young man to fall in love with her.

There's the plot. Watch, if you will,
How it develops. Please do.
Ah, here they come, I believe, and what do you think
They're talking about? Precisely so.
Love, about falling in love. (44–49)

   The Prologue opening is dramatic shorthand. In Plautus and Terence the function of the Prologue was often to secure a hearing. In the rough and tumble of a Roman festival where an audience could be, and not infrequently was, lost to rival attractions, the Prologue needed to guarantee quality; to assure the audience of a good time; to sound out the reception that the players in character could expect that day. The greater formality, which still in Menander's day surrounded the presentation of plays at the Great Dionysia and the Lenaia, preserved the playwright from the indignities suffered by Terence when his audience defected to a troupe of tightrope walkers. But if he wrote as many plays as logic would seem to suggest, for festivals that were less formal than the grand Athenian civic occasions, Menander might well have been advised to assume that an audience would be that much more attentive if they knew what was going to happen. That way they could always feel they were one step more clever than the clever people on stage.
   There is a point, too, about stage suspense. No great play, whether comic or tragic, depends on the audience's not knowing the outcome. Greek tragedy in the plays of Aeschylus, Sophocles, and Euripides offered a single viewing of each new piece. The treatment of any story might be individual but it was marked by the inevitability of certain givens. An audience attending Euripides' *Phoenician Women* and discovering, title notwithstanding, that the play was set in Thebes at the time of the civil war conducted by the sons of Oedipus and Jokasta, might have been reminded of Aeschylus' *Seven Against Thebes*, whose timescale it duplicates. They would surely have recalled Sophocles' *Oedipus Tyrannus* at the end of which Jocasta hangs herself and Oedipus is driven into exile while their sons, Eteokles and Polyneikes, are left behind in Thebes. The suspense, and indeed the shock effect, of *Phoenician Women* stemmed from how the story would be resolved in a Thebes which, in contrast to the Aeschylus and Sophocles treatments, still held a living Jokasta and a resident Oedipus. What the audience knew could never be changed was the resolution of the Theban civil war in which the two brothers would kill one another in hand-to-hand combat. Details could change; fundamentals could not.

Nor, in more recent times, would anyone be likely to claim that they had no intention of going to a *Merchant of Venice* or a *Much Ado About Nothing* on the grounds that they already knew that Portia would get Antonio off and Beatrice would end up marrying Benedick. Knowledge of the plot, especially in comedy, is no hindrance to its enjoyment.

What Menander's Prologue does do is set up the play's premise and point the audience toward its spine. In *The Malcontent*, it is primarily a matter of atmosphere. Knemon and his obsession are placed in the context of a love affair. If the nature of that love affair is something we must later confront in greater detail, at least the Prologue points to a sense of order and a sense of purpose.

The Woman from Samos also has a Prologue, delivered, not by a God but by one of the main characters, and occupying almost 8 percent of the whole play. This time it is the young man Moschion who is in a quandary. The opening is missing, but he has decided to share his problem with the audience. Two lines into the play as we have it, he decides to reveal all:

> Look, gentlemen (*to the audience*).
> I think it would be best if I were to tell you the whole story
> Beginning with the sort of man my father is.
> I remember my childhood as comfortable.
> Nothing more to say except that at the time
> I didn't realise how comfortable.
> At eighteen I was registered as a citizen
> In the ordinary way, "nem con" as they say,
> Though between ourselves my origins are somewhat humble,
> God knows. (*The Woman from Samos* 3–12)

Clearly, Moschion is an adopted son, though the particular circumstances are lost in the mutilated manuscript. The remainder of the Prologue speech has the same expositional purpose as has Pan in *The Malcontent*. The difference is that Pan is in control of the action, the playwright at work: the playwright as God, in effect, manipulating the characters, like George Bernard Shaw in the famous caricature as marionette-master.[5] By introducing one of those who is most involved in the action as Prologue for *The Woman from Samos*, Menander creates a wholly different tension.

Pan in *The Malcontent* has a single speech, a speech of reassurance, that lets the audience know that this is comedy, comfortable comedy, which is not likely to jump up and bite them when they least expect it. The misanthropy of the title character will give one comic drive, and the vicissitudes of a love affair will provide the other. The tone is secure. Whatever may happen, the playwright as God is in control, and all will be well that ends well. Menander does, as it happens, have one sting in his tail but the playwright's self-confidence, remarkable in what was such an early work, is catching. *The Malcontent* never becomes an anxious play.

The same cannot be said for *The Woman from Samos*. Moschion's nervousness is as infectious as is Pan's serenity. It makes its appearance from the first lines that we have, and it is hardly a rash inference to surmise that the missing opening lines showed him as tentative as does the surviving part of the speech. Moschion eventually succeeds in settling down sufficiently to be able to accomplish the Prologue's main task of introducing the audience to the background and the leading characters.

Moschion's father Demeas fell in love with Chrysis, a courtesan from Samos, and took her into his home as his mistress. Chrysis subsequently became pregnant, but Demeas was insistent that she should get rid of the child. As he could not legally marry Chrysis, any baby would be illegitimate. Demeas then went away to the Black Sea on business, taking with him his next-door neighbor Nikeratos, a poor man with a wife, Myrrhine, and a daughter, Plangon. In the absence of the two men, Chrysis became a close friend of Myrrhine. So far, so good.

At this point Moschion begins to get more and more uncomfortable. But he has undertaken to tell the audience exactly what has been going on, and so he does. One night he came home unexpectedly to find the two households celebrating the Festival of Adonis:

> There was lots of eating and drinking and fun and games—
> You know how it is—and because I'd come home anyway
> I couldn't resist going to have a look. . . .
> I'm not sure I want to tell you what happened next.
> Quite disgraceful, of course. But it's a bit late
> To worry about that. Still I am ashamed of myself.
> The girl got pregnant. There. I've told you the outcome.
> You can fill in the in between bit yourself. (38–42, 47–51)

Already this is on the way to becoming a comedy of intrigue, a concoction of misunderstandings and deceptions and the testing in the process of a whole number of slightly uneasy relationships. The remainder of Moschion's Prologue compounds the possibilities for confusion. He had declared that he wanted to marry the pregnant Plangon, but he could do nothing about it before the return of the two fathers. Meanwhile, Chrysis, the Samian, had her baby and, although she believed she could persuade Demeas to accept it, the baby apparently died. The gaps in the manuscript leave this detail unclear. Certainly, Chrysis is free and willing to wet-nurse Plangon's baby until such time as the two fathers can be persuaded to allow the marriage of Plangon and Moschion. Yet another complication is added over status and the sense of pride that goes with it. Nikeratos may be a friend of Demeas, but he is too poor to be able to provide his daughter with a dowry.

The last piece of information Moschion appears to have offered, in another mutilated section of this most complex of jigsaws, is that Demeas and Nikeratos's ship has been sighted. The characters are set on a collision course that is the product of loving but not wholly trusting relationships. Despite all the missing sections—barely half the speech survives—the playwright has contrived to build up a picture of character and situation that sets a pattern for everything that is to come. Here is no cosy study of lovable grotesques but a full-blown, lively drama propelled by a sense of urgency and real human feeling. The full extent of this will be considered in the next chapter when we analyze how far situations are driven by character in these two plays. For the present it is enough to note that any disappointment expressed over the two Menander plays when they were discovered was misplaced and that the criticisms since of such commentators as Allinson and Tarn are dismally unimaginative.[6] Both plays are the work of a natural dramatist who from the outset of his career gives every evidence of having been a master technician.

The tendency to set up the play's frame of reference from its Prologue was one of the few features of Menander's technique which could be tested, albeit sporadically, from the major fragmentary plays that in the first half of the century constituted the surviving corpus. Unfortunately, *The Arbitration* lacks most of its first act, but later indications in the text point to a Prologue from a deity. As much of the play as does survive suggests pattern and purpose, a sense of divinity biding its time until mere mortals stop chasing their tails and get on with the process of living. The series of coincidences whereby the baby is conceived, born, exposed, rescued, and finally restored to its parents is treated with a kind of naive wonder by the characters. This is a nice contrast to Ion's frank skepticism in Euripides's earlier tragicomedy. The theme has all the hallmarks of the classic comic situation.

The proposal that the lost Act One did contain a Prologue from some appropriate deity is strengthened by the reaction of Charisios, the husband, at the moment in Act Four when he comes to see his hypocrisy:

> A decent man, that's how I saw myself,
> A proper moral judge of right and wrong,
> So "without stain" in my own life.

Well, some Power above (*daimonion*) has put me in my place
and shown me as I am.
"You thrice-cursed brute," says the Power,
"With all your airs and talk." (*The Arbitration* 908–14)

The slave Onesimos in Act Five offers his view that the world is far too large for God to care about everyone, and then he continues:

Is God not bothered about the individual then?
Of course he is. He gives us each a guardian angel
And that guardian angel is our character,
Deep down inside us. That's our God. (1092–96)

The Shorn Girl (*Perikeiromene*) appears to have a similar structure. The first lines we possess are delivered by *Agnoia*, the personification of Ignorance or Mistake. This is an accurate enough guide to the likely direction of the comedy. *The Shorn Girl* or, as in some versions, *The Rape of the Locks,* deals with the misunderstanding created when a Corinthian soldier, Polemon, finds Glykera, the young girl he has been given to look after by someone he believes to be her mother, being embraced by another man in the street. In his fury he hauls her back home and cuts off her hair. What Polemon does not know is that the man embracing Glykera was her long-lost brother, Moschion. The extra dimension to what cannot but appear as something of a sleazy tale is that, although Glykera knew that it was her long-lost brother who was doing the embracing, Moschion did not know that she was his sister and was apparently embracing in the street a total stranger whom he happened to like the look of. Menander, however, is not so simple.

All this has been stirred up," continues Ignorance,
For the future and to put him (Polemon) into a rage.
I've led him on, contrary to his nature,
To help the business of discovery
And get on with the recognition.
So if anyone was dismayed or found that scene offensive
Reconsider. Bad turns to good when a God does the driving,
(*The Shorn Girl* 162–70).

Behind this neat reversal, engineered at the expense of the audience, is a cunning piece of craftsmanship. The above line-numbering for the end of the Prologue shows that the play opened with a substantial scene, a scene of some 120 lines, *before* the Prologue. That early scene may have featured the meeting of Moschion and Glykera or, more probably, a report of it and Polemon's anguished response. At any rate it seems to have been a harsh scene, a scene barely appropriate to a comedy at all, which only the magic wand of the playwright can transform into the stuff of comedy. The whole first scene was apparently a kind of "pre-credit" sequence, with the audience in the dark about who the characters were and what was going on. Only once the tragic potential of the play has been established does the God/playwright put in an appearance.

The mood that this juxtaposition of scenes would seem to inspire is one of misapprehension compounded by human failing. Polemon's fury is, we must believe, real enough; Glykera's humiliation is something worse, until the playwright turns up to let his characters off the hook and set up, by the end of Act Five, reconciliations and apologies all around. Ignorance, as Prologue, is initially a compounder of misfortune. The old woman who had rescued brother and sister when exposed as infants had informed Glykera of her background but, for no identifiable reason, had failed to do the same for her brother: "She wanted to take care that she should never, through me—Ignorance, that's me—get into an improper relationship With him" (140–41).

Thus is Ignorance introduced to the audience as a troublesome figure, an image that is softened by the end of the speech in which she (*Agnoia* is a feminine noun) overturns the play's somewhat somber opening tone. And so the play is allowed to proceed on its own terms, with any potential savagery disarmed by the playwright's *apologia* and the audience's consequent complicity.

The Shield (*Aspis*) employs a similar device, but here the opening scene has survived. The play begins with the entry of Daos, former Tutor to the supposedly late Kleostratos, assumed killed in Lycia where he had been fighting as a mercenary. The stage picture of the return of the effects of a dead hero is compounded by a procession of the spoils of war, prisoners, mules loaded with booty, and Kleostratos' shield which Daos is carrying. Daos informs Smikrines, Kleostratos' uncle, of the circumstances surrounding his nephew's death. This early exchange contains little indication that the play is a comedy. Daos offers a funeral oration, lamenting the spoiled hopes of the dead man and his reasonable concerns for himself with his master gone.

Smikrines asks what happened, soliciting the grim reply: "For a soldier death's easy enough. Survival is the problem" (21–22). Daos proceeds to tell the story of the battle. Without having a date for the first production of the play, we have no means of knowing whether he is referring to an actual engagement. During the time that Menander was writing and presenting plays, there was no lack of military action around the river Xanthos, but if Menander wanted to recall in the mind of his audience a real battle, he has an oblique way of going about it. Specific or not, Daos' description of camp living and the vicissitudes of a mercenary's life must have rung a bell with many of those in the audience: and uncomfortably at that. Daos tells of looting villages, burning crops, and acquiring all the spoils which formed the opening procession. He proceeds to uncover the whole military operation. The natives had regrouped on hearing from deserters that the invaders were scattered. Kleostratos and the others were celebrating their victory when hit by a surprise sally. The chaos and confusion of a night attack gives way to retreat and a return three days later to find the fallen. Kleostratos' shield is found alongside a mutilated body. Daos has made his way home with whatever he could manage. "All this is yours," he says to Smikrines, pointing to the prisoners-of-war and to the booty. To which Smikrines replies: "I'm bothered with none of it. If only he had lived" (89–90).

The scene clears, and Daos and Smikrines are replaced by *Tuche*, Chance or Lady Luck, with the delayed Prologue. Her first lines immediately lighten the atmosphere:

> Well. If a real disaster had struck these people
> You could hardly have a god like me coming on next.
> They've no idea what really happened.
> They're floundering in the dark. (97–99)

The Greek translated here as "they've no idea what really happened" is *agnoousi*—literally "they are in ignorance" as *Agnoia* is the goddess of Ignorance whose delayed Prologue sets up *The Shorn Girl*.

Chance proceeds by telling what really happened. In the confusion of the night attack, someone picked up Smikrines' shield. Smikrines was subsequently captured but has now been released and is on his way home: nothing, in fact, that the audience might not have anticipated. Then, as a Prologue must, Chance begins to introduce the characters around whom the play will develop up to the arrival of Kleostratos, *ex mortuis*, if not *ex machina*, to sort everything out. The last half of the play is missing, but it is reasonable to assume that Menander had a surprise or two up his sleeve for Acts Four and Five.

The plot revolves around Smikrines, who asked all the questions of Daos, and his younger brother Chaerestratos, uncles of the supposedly dead Kleostratos. Chaerestratos has a daughter, Kleostratos a sister, and when Kleostratos went away to the wars, Chaerestratos brought up both together.

Chaerestratos was going to arrange for the sister's marriage to his stepson and give her the dowry her brother could not afford. According to Athenian law, however, the death of the brother makes Smikrines the nearest male relative and entitles him to marry his niece, divorcing his own wife in the process if necessary.[7] Seeing as his niece has become an heiress, she becomes an attractive proposition, and the intrigue of the play revolves around attempts to thwart Smikrines, attempts that the god's eye view of the audience knows will be rendered redundant the moment the "dead" Kleostratos puts in his appearance.

More important is the rider posed by Chance that in the process Smikrines' hypocrisy will be revealed for all the world to see. The situation is largely an excuse, albeit a good dramatic one, for the exposure of a villain. It is only at this late stage that Chance reveals her identity:

> All that remains is to tell you my name.
> I'm mistress of ceremonies here. I'm in control. I'm *Tuche*.
>   (146–48)

The revelation that the core of the play is the character of Smikrines throws interesting extra light on the opening scene. Serious and unrelieved as is Daos' account—and there is no reason to believe that the playwright intended the actor to "send up" the scene—there is the character of Smikrines to be considered. In contrast to any suggestion that Daos should not play straight, there are good grounds for allowing the audience to see through Smikrines in this opening scene.

Initially, Smikrines is cast as the recipient of Daos' sorry tale. His early exchanges are what you would expect of the subsidiary character in any expositional duologue. As soon as Daos mentions that everyone in the army came back from a raid with plenty of money, however, Smikrines' ears begin to twitch: "That's nice." Daos eventually gets to the end of his account. What is Smikrines' reaction?

SMIKRINES: Is that six hundred gold crowns you said you'd brought home?

DAOS: Yes.

SMIKRINES: Silver cups too?

DAOS: Forty minas' worth, that's all. You're the heir.

SMIKRINES: What do you mean? Do you think that's why I'm asking? God in heaven! Everything else taken, was it?

DAOS: Most of it. Except what I reached first. There are some tunics and cloaks. And this crowd, of course (*indicating the slaves*).

SMIKRINES: I'm bothered with none of it. If only he had lived. (82–90)

This response of Smikrines, taken out of context, could be considered the sympathetic response from a grieving relative, but in the light of the rest of the exchange it appears more revealing. The signal to the audience to pay attention to Smikrines comes in the planting of the single response "That's nice." From such a seed is born the crafty miser who sits spider-like at the heart of *The Shield*. This is a masterful opening and makes it all the more regrettable that there is as yet no way of knowing the resolution.

Much of the opening sequences of *The Farmer* (*Georgos*), *The Sikyonian* (*Sikuonios*), and *The Man She Hated* (*Misoumenos*) survive reinforcing the sense of craft with which Menander set up his opening scenes. To consider the construction of whole plays we have recourse only to the two plays that can be treated as virtually complete.

Both *The Malcontent* and *The Woman from Samos* have a five-act structure. *The Malcontent* is widely assumed to be an early piece. That may make *The Woman from Samos* a more mature play. In most respects this seems fair comment, although the lukewarm reception initially accorded to the rediscovery of *The Malcontent* reflects more on the expectations of its detractors than on its intrinsic merits as a stage piece. As it stands, *The Malcontent* reveals a sophistication in construction and in the handling of a large cast which belies its reputation as fledgling work.

At the end of Pan's Prologue the young man Sostratos, whom Pan has caused to fall in love with Knemon's daughter, makes his entrance with a parasite, Chaereas. The parasite is a stock secondary character who might be expected to help resolve problems encountered by the central characters. Here he serves as the recipient for Sostratos's lament about being in love. This function could have been performed by Sostratos' slave Pyrrhias, but Menander holds Pyrrhias back for a "running slave" entrance.[8] What has happened is that Sostratos has already sent Pyrrhias off earlier in the morning to see Knemon and tell him that his master has fallen in love with her.

Even Sostratos, not the most intelligent of characters, does not need Cheareas to make him aware that this was not the best way to go about soliciting her hand. The entry of Pyrrhias quickens the tempo of the play as he rushes in, eager to tell the world how Knemon chased him off after pelting him with clods of earth and stones for daring to encroach on his land. All this is too much for Chaereas whose enthusiasm for helping out rapidly evaporates. He beats a retreat and never returns to the play. He has served his purpose and enabled the playwright to complete the exposition begun in the god-Prologue and rounded off by the introduction of the young lover.

Sostratos naturally blames Pyrrhias for mishandling the situation. Pyrrhias catches sight of Knemon and heads off; Pyrrhias, in all probability, never returns either. This is certainly an unusual opening. In the first 150 lines of the first act, four characters have been introduced and three of them have left never to return. This might have been one feature of a restricted number of actors, an issue already raised in Chapter 3. It may simply be a way of clearing the decks, as it were, for the first meeting of the two men whose contrary natures give the play its comic momentum.

The expected encounter hardly happens. Knemon is so busy fulminating against the world at large that he assumes that Sostratos is just another gossip rather than the real threat to his stability that Sostratos is about to prove:

KNEMON: Is there no privacy? You couldn't find a quiet spot to commit suicide.

SOSTRATOS: Is it me he's annoyed with? (*to Knemon*) I arranged to meet someone here, old chap. Just waiting for him.

KNEMON: What did I tell you? What do you think this is, a pedestrian precinct? The War Memorial? Use my front door, why don't you, if you want to arrange an assignation? Why don't I change it all about? Dedicate a bench? No, wait. I'll have a shelter built. You can use it as your headquarters. It hurts, you know that? Persecution, that's what I call it.

Exit Knemon (*The Malcontent* 169–78)

So the combination of sarcasm on the one hand and diffidence on the other ensures that the initial confrontation fails properly to materialize. Knemon, in other words, does not discover that his daughter has a suitor, nor does he know that his security is under attack. One potential direction for the play to take has been set up and promptly discarded. Either Knemon or Sostratos is on-stage for most of the rest of the play, but they do not meet again until Act Four. Sostratos gets in on Knemon's rescue after Knemon falls down the well—but in such a ham-fisted fashion, by his own account, that he can hardly have furthered his suit. Eventually, Gorgias, Knemon's stepson, does introduce Sostratos as a part-rescuer and prospective son-in-law, but by this time Knemon is so demoralized by his experiences down the well that he has abdicated any decisions relating to the future of his daughter or his estate.

Avoiding this potential source of a comic scene is no evasion. It enables the emphasis of the play to remain on the central character and his person-ality. It is certainly the mark of a confident and sustained dramatist who is not prepared to take the easy route.

Having rejected the big scene between Knemon and Sostratos in Act One, Menander now introduces the daughter. Apparently, the playwright has so little interest in this daughter as an individual that he has never got around to giving her a name. The plotline, which is often intermittent, now takes a step forward. The Daughter cannot fetch water from her well because the servant Simiche has dropped the bucket down the well. Sostratos offers to fill her a pitcher from the shrine and is so overcome when she says "thank you" that he goes all weak at the knees. So the love interest is established and working well. So is the sense of complication, for the act ends with Gorgias' slave, Daos, catching sight of Sostratos' encounter with the Daughter and deciding something must be done about it.

Act Two consolidates the action. The new character is Gorgias, stepson to Knemon and living in the house on the other side of Pan's shrine. Daos tells him what he has seen, and the arrival of Sostratos enables Gorgias to confront him. Discovering that Sostratos' intentions are honorable, Gorgias agrees to help, though he is still wary of Sostratos' wealth in the light of his own poverty. The plan he devises for Sostratos to impress Knemon by the diligence of his digging in Gorgias' fields is hardly disinterested. Sostratos and Gorgias leave for the country to be replaced by a Cook, Sikon. A scene of character contrast is succeeded by a low-comedy scene between Cook and the slave Getas.

Knemon opens Act Three by confronting at the shrine of Pan the Sacrificial Party which has been initiated by Sostratos' mother and her entourage. Two scenes follow in which Knemon, having decided he dare not leave his house unguarded with so many suspicious people about, runs the gauntlet of first Getas and then Sikon, as they try to borrow cooking utensils. Sending them packing provokes their revenge in Act Five when, with Knemon too injured to retaliate, they persecute him in a scene that might appear vicious were it not mirrored by this earlier rejection of their own requests for assistance.

The departure of the Cook is the signal for the return of Sostratos, stiff and sunburned but resolved as much as ever to invoke Gorgias' help by inviting him to join the family celebrations. At this point the plot proper gets another nudge with the entrance of Knemon's old servant Simiche who has now lost the spade down the well while trying to fish out the bucket she had dropped in earlier. All these aggravations seem calculated to enrage Knemon who threatens to throw Simiche after bucket and spade, but then resolves to climb down after them himself. The various strands of the story overlap more and more as Sostratos issues his party invitation to Gorgias and the third act ends.

Predictably enough, Act Four opens with Simiche bringing the news that Knemon has now fallen down the well. The various slaves and the Cook are not oversympathetic, and it is left to Gorgias to get the old man out, with Sostratos giving nominal assistance, as he records when informing the audience what happened:

> We had no sooner got inside than Gorgias launched himself down the well after him. And I was up there with the girl and we didn't have to do anything. I mean, what could we do? She was tearing her hair out, of course, and beating her breast a lot. And there was I comforting her, the knight in shining armour—I was, I swear I was—and saying "There, there" and "Never mind" and just staring at this vision. I didn't care two hoots about the victim. Except that I had to haul him out. That was a bit of a bore. Especially as I was so busy looking at the girl, I kept letting go of the rope. Three times, anyway. Gorgias was a positive Atlas. He hung on like grim death and eventually, after a great deal of effort, got him out. (669–84)

The remainder of the play revolves around Knemon's reaction to his experiences, which is discussed more suitably in the next chapter when considering Menander's handling of character. Knemon retires to his house after handing over all his affairs, including the disposal of his daughter, to Gorgias. The arrival of Sostratos' father seems to set up an ending that is satisfactory all around. As in *The Woman from Samos*, however, Menander has something up his sleeve for Act Five. First, there is a revealing scene between Gorgias, Sostratos, and Sostratos' father in which questions of pride and poverty almost prevent Gorgias from agreeing to marry Sostratos' sister. When all this has been satisfactorily resolved, there follows the persecution of Knemon, the playing of which is considered elsewhere. Knemon is finally persuaded to join in the wedding party, and the play ends with the slave Getas appealing for applause and the prize.

The blend of subtle and farcical, plot-led and character-led scenes, is crafted with considerable skill, as much for what is left untapped as for what is made a part of the play's structure. The play's dramatic rhythm is impeccable. "I wish, kid, that this was not such a noisy play" was Sam Harris's immortal advice to Moss Hart after the initial tryouts of *Once in a Lifetime* had shown a diminishing audience appreciation as the play reached its climax. "I think one of the main things wrong with it is that it tires an audience out." It turned out to be the only thing wrong with *Once in a Lifetime*. The subsequent inclusion of a quiet scene late in the play with two people sitting and talking on a train gave the audience a breather and turned the play into a smash hit. Menander could write a noisy scene. He knew better than to write a noisy play.

The initial anxiety created in *The Woman from Samos* by Moschion delivering the Prologue to the audience as an involved party does impart a sense of urgency to the proceedings. Moschion is then involved in the first scene proper which introduces two of the other principals, the slave Parmenon and Chrysis, the Samian herself. Parmenon is exasperated, and Chrysis is the calming influence who assumes that she can work everything out. Moschion departs, eventually to find a quiet place to rehearse what he is going to say to his father Demeas.

Demeas is thereby set up as a man with a short fuse, but his arrival from the trip abroad with his poor neighbor Nikeratos shows the two older men in a different light. They are simply pleased to be back, and they are all the happier for having arranged between them that Moschion should marry Nikeratos' daughter Plangon. Here the first act ends, neatly set up as a comedy of misunderstanding. All parties in the play are striving for the same end. The confusions multiply because no one is aware of what anyone else has in mind.

Act Two begins with the entrance of a very different Demeas. The first thing he has seen upon reentering his house is Chrysis nursing a baby, a baby that he naturally assumes to be his. Far from avoiding a meeting between father and son at this point, Menander immediately engineers it. By this time, Chrysis' plan to pretend the baby is hers rather than Plangon's is too far advanced to explain, and all Moschion can do is attempt to deflect Demeas' anger away from Chrysis. There is a gap in the text here, but by the end Demeas has broached the subject of Moschion's proposed marriage and is delighted to discover that Moschion is overjoyed. Moschion departs, but Nikeratos arrives to say that his family has given the news a subdued reception. There is another hiatus, but it seems he never got around to explaining to Plangon and her mother who the prospective bridegroom is. Demeas will have none of that and for the second act in succession, everything seems to be running smoothly, with only the slightest of hiccups or potential hiccups.

Act Three opens with a long speech from Demeas in which he relates what he saw and heard indoors, which has now led him to believe not only that the baby belongs to Chrysis, but also that his son Moschion is the father and that everyone except him seems to know it. At this point, almost incongruously, Menander introduces one of the ubiquitous Cooks without which, it seems, no New Comedy would be complete.

The Cook has a double function. Initially, he serves to give the slave Parmenon a stage focus other than that of his social superiors. Later in the act, when Parmenon has appeared to confirm Demeas' worst suspicions,

Demeas confronts Chrysis. The scene again revolves around Demeas declining to put into words exactly what he thinks has happened, which leaves Chrysis with no charge to refute. More importantly for the play, Demeas' callousness is set against a ridiculous backdrop, as we have already seen when considering the staging of the scene in Chapter 3, by the presence of the Cook whose periodic interference contrasts with the scene's serious content. The neighbor Nikeratos restores a comic tempo by taking Chrysis in and suggesting that Demeas' anger is only temporary and will soon pass.

This conciliatory end to Act Three leads into the next confrontation of father and son and more harsh words from Demeas whose constant claim "I know everything" is taken at face value by everyone to whom he addresses it. The presence of Nikeratos compounds the confusion as he too gets it into his head that Chrysis is the baby's mother and Moschion the father. He stamps off into his house leaving the scene for Moschion at last to gather what Demeas has suspected. Moschion confesses that he is indeed the father of the baby but that Plangon is the mother. Demeas is not entirely convinced until Nikeratos returns with news of what he has just seen:

DEMEAS: Whatever's the matter?

NIKERATOS: Giving the baby a tit. I just saw her, my daughter, in my house.

DEMEAS: Probably a joke.

NIKERATOS: It was no joke. As soon as she saw me, she collapsed in a heap.

DEMEAS: She probably thought . . .

NIKERATOS: What's all this "probably" all the time? (539–44)

Suddenly we are back in the realm of a comedy double-act after a dangerous flirtation with something more painful. This blend of the comic with the potentially serious is, I have few doubts, the cornerstone of Menander's stage technique. He makes it possible, if not inevitable, for characters to suffer in the silliest or most mundane of circumstances and frequently in the presence of other characters who react in the most eccentric of ways. At this moment it is Nikeratos who is suffering agonies at the thought of his daughter having had an illegitimate child. Looking for sympathy, he discovers his best friend delighted at the proof that it is his son who is the father.

Chrysis is now thrown out of Nikeratos' house and, after the most perfunctory of reconciliations with Demeas, a farcical scene ensues with the two old men almost coming to blows. Demeas offers Nikeratos a wholly preposterous divine explanation of how Plangon might have become pregnant. Nikeratos is not convinced, but Demeas diverts him into a couple of jokes at the expense of local celebrities and all ends in reconciliation. This is by far the most complex and varied single act in surviving Menander. It is written exclusively in trochees rather than iambics, suggesting pace and drive despite the extreme variations of mood. The sequence of entrances and exits is a further indication of technical virtuosity:

421 *Enter Nikeratos*

428 *Enter Moschion*

440 *Enter Demeas*

520 *Exit Nikeratos*

532 *Enter Nikeratos*

539 *Exit Moschion*

547 *Exit Nikeratos*

556 *Enter Nikeratos*

563 *Exit Nikeratos*

568 *Enter Chrysis from Nikeratos' house*

570 *Enter Nikeratos*

575 *Exit Chrysis to Demeas' house*

614 *Exit Nikeratos*

615 *Exit Demeas*

The end of Act Four would appear to leave the plot wrapped up, but Menander offers a change of direction. Now that Moschion has got over his fright, it begins to dawn on him what his father believed had happened. He decides to teach him a lesson by pretending to leave home. The true reconciliation scene will be examined in detail in the next chapter, but father and son do come to terms. The play ends with Moschion's marriage to Plangon and a customary appeal for the prize.

The sophistication involved in creating characters who learn from experience and change for the better is the aspect of character-drawing to which we must now turn.

NOTES

1. *Moralia* 854 B.C. For the whole essay, see Appendix 1.
2. Edited by F. H. Sandbach, Oxford: Oxford University Press, 1972.
3. Introduction to *Aristophanes and Menander: New Comedy*, London: Methuen, 1994, pp. xxvi ff.

4. Manchester: Manchester University Press, 1950, 2nd ed., 1960, Appendix, pp. 220–34.

5. Cf. Norwood's *Euripides and Shaw*, London: Methuen, 1921.

6. See Chapter 3, p. 45.

7. For a good summary of such laws in Athens and the impact on women's lives, see Elaine Fantham's article, "Sex, Status and Survival in Hellenistic Athens: A Study of Women in New Comedy," in *Phoenix* 29, 1975. pp. 44–74.

8. The running slave was a familiar character in New Comedy whose function within the action was largely rhythmical, offering a burst of physical action to follow a more static sequence of dialogue.

Chapter 5

Menander's People

In his summary of the differences between Aristophanes and Menander, Plutarch complains of Aristophanes that "He doles out whatever language turns up to any character as though handing it out by lot. There is no way of telling whether someone is a father or a son from what they say, a yokel or a god, an old woman or a hero." Plutarch prefers Menander whose diction "is so smooth and consistent that he manages to adapt it to the whole range of emotions, personalities and character traits"[1]

F. H. Sandbach has pointed out[2] that this could either mean that Menander had found a single style for all his characters or that he had found a style appropriate for each individual character. Sandbach inclines to the second view. Although a case might be made as in so many areas for Euripides having led the way, this would make Menander the first playwright to have created characters who are distinguishable by the way in which they speak. Any close reading of the texts suggests that Sandbach is right.

Such an approach to stage writing might suggest that for Menander and, perhaps to a lesser extent, other authors of New Comedy, character had overtaken plot as the main feature of the drama. Aristotle (384–322 B.C.) in the *Poetics* had stated that the reverse was true for tragedy.[3] The move to a new priority for character was heralded by Theophrastus (c.370–c.287 B.C.), who was not a playwright but Aristotle's successor as the head of the Peripatetic School in Athens and the inheritor of his library. One of Theophrastus' own pupils was Menander.

Theophrastus wrote prolifically, if not as prolifically as Aristotle, on a whole range of topics. Not a great deal survives, but there is one light work entitled *Characters* which offers an incomparable gallery of Athenian types, several of whom find, and many of whom might have found, their way into the plays and fragments of the pupil he managed to outlive.

These characters all have a title such as *eiron*, the dissembler, *alazon*, the boaster, *kolax*, the flatterer. Not only do they provide moulds for many of the peripheral personalities who haunt the fringes of the plays, but also they sometimes offer a basis for leading roles. Consider Theophrastus' *Mikrologos*, the Miser, who "will subtract the cost from a slave's food allowance if he breaks some old pot. . . . Nobody can pick up a fig from his garden or as much as walk across his land. . . . He refuses to let his wife lend a neighbour salt, lampwick or herbs. . . . 'It all mounts up, you know, in a year.' "[4]: and *Authades*, the Surly Fellow, who "asked where someone is, replies 'No business of mine' and, if you bid him good morning, doesn't deign to reply. . . . He curses the stone he trips over. Can't bear being kept waiting: is never prepared to sing, to recite or to dance. As like as not, he doesn't pray to the gods either" (XV). Between these two, do we not find Knemon, the central figure of *The Malcontent*?

What a wealth of dramatic material is afforded by the Tactless Man who "if he becomes involved in an arbitration sets the parties to blows just when they've reached agreement"; the Coward who "hides his sword under his pillow so he can spend an age looking for it"; or the Mean Man who "spots a friend who is raising a subscription and takes the sidestreets home to avoid him." Theophrastus offers a full range of human foibles in neat pen-sketches.

There is a contradiction here, however, one that needs to be addressed before we look in more detail at individual characters or character types. On the one hand, there is the association of Menander with stock figures—misers, dissemblers, parasites—never mind the recurrent professionals—cooks, soldiers, and courtesans—all of whom seem to be defined by a restricted range of human activities and a still more restricted way of reacting to them. The scope for some characters is limited by function. Every character faces limitations imposed by Athenian society whose social conventions, notably those of status and gender, make it hard to imagine how any playwright found plots enough for a hundred plays. Terence's comments in the Prologue of his *The Girl from Andros*—that Menander had written two plays, *The Girl from Andros* and *The Girl from Perinthos*, and that to all intents and purposes the plots were identical—reinforces the supposition. So does the whole series of arguments over plagiarism, confusing as they may be, which seem to have plagued Plautus and Terence in their Latin adaptations throughout their careers.

Against this is posed the longstanding tradition in the ancient world that Menander's plays were positively naturalistic, so true to life that they were indistinguishable from the real thing: and particularly staged in a theatre whose physical features made realism far from easy. The description "naturalistic" is to be used with caution, of course, for in contemporary parlance it relates more to form than to content. There is still an assumption that Menander was successful, in a way that no other playwright of the ancient world could rival, in depicting real issues and real situations. Because the "real" world of contemporary politics is never allowed to intrude and the uncomfortable questions of abuse, sickness, or corruption remain sidelined, what reality there is exists within structured family relationships and their complexities. This must account for human frailty rather than human viciousness lying at the heart of most dramatic situations.

The nearest to a real villain in the admittedly scanty remains of Menander would appear to be Smikrines in *The Shield* whom Chance in the Prologue describes as "exceeding all men in knavery. He recognises neither relation nor friend, shrinks from no dishonesty and wants everything for himself" (*The Shield* 116–20). That would seem to be fairly unequivocal. Chance, as a god, has no personal axe to grind. If she declares Smikrines a knave, then knave he must surely be, in whose comeuppance by the end of the play the entire audience can delight. With so little of *The Shield* surviving, we cannot know by what means that is achieved, of course, but one suggestion from W. G. Arnott[5] is that the Cook and the slave Daos perpetrate an act of revenge on Smikrines at a time when everyone except Smikrines has become aware of Kleostratos' return from the dead.

The parallel to *The Malcontent* is close but feasible.

Knemon too finds much of the last act devoted to his discomfiture at the hands of a Cook and a Slave. The Prologue, Pan, introduces Knemon to the audience as Tuche introduces Smikrines:

> Here to my right, your left, lives Knemon,
> A malcontent, if ever there was one,
> Hostile to allcomers, cranky in a crowd.
> "In a crowd?" did I say? never in his life
> Has this Knemon volunteered a friendly word
> To anyone, never made overtures to a living soul:
> Bar me, and with Pan as a neighbour, he has little option.
> He can hardly ignore a god and pass him by,

Though that upsets him for the day, I have no doubt.
(*The Malcontent* 5–13)

Pan continues in the same vein as he describes Knemon's unfortunate and short-lived marriage during which his wife bore him a daughter before moving out:

"The old man has a daughter," he concludes,
"But otherwise lives alone
Except for a woman slave, older than he is.
All his days are working days, digging, carting wood
And hating everyone in sight, his wife, his neighbours,
In a ten mile radius, down to the very last, the lot."
(29–34)

Thus set up, the audience is prepared for the worst. Sostratos, who has fallen in love with Knemon's daughter, courtesy of Pan, is in for a rough ride. Knemon's reputation is already at rock bottom, but the actions of others in the cast are hardly helpful. Sostratos, instead of approaching the father himself to ask for the girl's hand, sends a tactless slave. The treatment of women as commodities will be considered below, but at least there is some difference between a slave and a freeborn girl. A rich young man should never approach the daughter of a respectable farmer, albeit a poor and crusty one, by means of a slave, as though this were some commercial proposition. "Oh dear, oh dear," says Chaireas, a professional fixer. "Yes, it wasn't very clever, I see that," replies Sostratos. "It's not really a job for a slave. Love and judgement are poor bedfellows" (74–79). The arrival into the action of Pyrrhias, the slave in question, endorses Knemon's hostile response to strangers. Pyrrhias' sense of propriety has left something to be desired. Instead of approaching Knemon by the path, he has walked straight across Knemon's field before stopping a little way off and shouting: "Oy, Dad, I've come on business and I'm in a hurry" (107–8). Small wonder that Knemon chased him off, pelting him with pears. Even Sostratos can see that: "You damaged his land. Pinched something probably" (142).

Such justifications are not intended to let Knemon off the hook. A playwright is not going to write a play called *The Malcontent* and then show his title character as a paragon of virtue. They do suggest, surely, that Menander is intent on setting Knemon up as something other than a cipher whose behavior and language are dictated by a single inflicted trait. Yes, Knemon's misanthropy is the catalyst to action, comic action

at that, but his sense of grievance turns to social satire the moment he
has a point. His nature as a "solitary" then comes under the microscope
too. In Menander there is room for such analysis. Knemon has some of
the qualities of Shakespeare's Jacques as well as of his Timon. His dislike
of people: "Is there no privacy? You couldn't find a quiet spot to commit
suicide" (170), is the product of the way of the world, a noisy and
thoughtless world from which he prefers to try to live in exile. But even
a Knemon is not an island, as the play proceeds to demonstrate: nor is it
fair to require others to share an obsession. There's a message there that
has not dimmed with time.

Knemon does not put in his next appearance until Act Three. He is
about to leave for work when the sacrificial party begins to arrive at Pan's
shrine. His immediate concern for his own property is again transformed
into satire when he turns on the reasons for having such sacrifices:

> They come with their sunbeds and their bottles of wine. It's all for their
> benefit, nothing to do with the gods. One pinch of incense, a crumb of holy
> cake, thanks very much, that'll do for piety. It all goes on the fire, so that's
> good enough for the gods. Oh, and the gods can have the extremities and the
> gall-bladder, anything that humans find inedible. Then they pitch in and
> polish off the good bits. (447–53)

This is a remarkable speech, not only because of its sentiments, worthy
of a Juvenal, but also because it both justifies and begins to account for
Knemon's attitudes. For a lot of the time he is correct in assuming that the
world is interested only in getting something out of him. So he sees off the
outsiders, the slave and the Cook who come to borrow pots and pans, for
the time being, but meanwhile his domestic affairs are beginning to gang
up on him. His bucket is down the well, and Simiche has dropped his spade
in after it. Tempted to throw her in too, he resists, only to fall in himself
when he tries to retrieve them. The ensuing rescue offers the playwright two
obvious possibilities. One is that Knemon will be so chastened by his
experience that he will turn over a new leaf and everyone will live happily
ever after. The other is that he won't but that some device will be found by
which his daughter and Sostratos can get married. Of the two, Menander
naturally opts for the latter, but with some refinements that again give
grounds for treating him as a playwright with something serious to say about
the world.

The long speech he delivers to his former wife and Gorgias, the stepson
who has rescued him, is precocious in its psychology:

I was wrong about one thing, I suppose. I thought I was the only person in the world who was self-sufficient. I thought that I didn't need people. Now I've stared death in the face and know he can turn up when you least expect him. My mistake and I admit it. Everyone needs a helping hand sometime. You see, I'd lost my faith in human nature. I'd watched how friendship had become no more than a commodity with a calculated profit margin. And I assumed that the same was true for all relationships everywhere. It was like a physical barrier. (713–22)

This speech is hardly that of the incorrigible recluse to whom Pan has introduced us in his Prologue. The desire to absent oneself from human contact may have greater intrinsic appeal than the miserliness of a Smik-rines, but it may have happened that, once *The Shield* reached its last act, Menander found a way of absolving Smikrines, allowing him to emerge as more tolerable than seems possible in our fragmented view.

Knemon continues by abdicating all responsibility for finding his daughter a husband in a touching confession to Gorgias: "Find her a husband. I couldn't do that. Nobody would ever be good enough for her" (732–34). There are moments when what we are shown of Sostratos makes us as an audience wonder whether he is not right and that Sostratos, anyway, is not good enough for her. It is not, I think, too far-fetched to think that this might be a contributory cause to Menander's reluctance to give the girl any real personality.

The speech ends with Knemon's declaration of faith:

I don't believe in wasting words, so I'll just say this.
I'd like you to understand why I am as I am. If everyone
behaved as I do, the lawcourt would be redundant; we
wouldn't need prisons; and there'd be an end to war.
Everyone would be content with his lot. (741–45)

The fifth act offers a change of key, back to the more robust style of the early play. In the new sympathetic light in which Knemon has been portrayed in Act Four, the means taken first to humiliate him and then to drive him into the wedding feast would be almost too much to stomach were the play to depend on a single tone. The writing is more complex than that, allowing a place for sentiment without forcing the play into sentimentality.

The extent to which Knemon's personality is developed in *The Mal-content* may come as a surprise to those who are expecting all the characters to be defined by the limited range of characteristics that the range of masks implies. A playwright of Menander's sympathies proves capable of taking a Theophrastian thumbnail sketch and creating from it a comparatively complex personality. *The Malcontent* also seems to demonstrate that such an approach is not taken to all characters. Apart from Knemon and perhaps Gorgias, the rest are largely ciphers. Slaves slave with reluctance, cook and parasite serve their turn without suggesting anything that does not promote the play's broader concerns, namely, the love affair of Sostratos and the personality of Knemon. In other words, as far as depth of character is concerned, Menander can be subtle but he is also selective.

Gorgias is something of an enigma here. One way of treating him would be to see him simply as an enabler, Pan's earthly surrogate, arriving in the right place at the right time to ensure that everything turns out as it should. Perhaps, however, there is something more than this, the founding of a moral position which puts Knemon's antisocial nature into perspective. Gorgias first appears at the beginning of Act Two, reprimanding the slave Daos for failing to take more positive action in defense of Knemon's daughter when he saw Sostratos talking to her: "She is my sister, for god's sake, and as far as you're concerned, that makes her family. . . . Her scandal would be our scandal" (239–43).

When he does catch sight of Sostratos, he accosts him and delivers a most curious homily full of aphorisms and pompous platitudes about wealth and poverty: the bluster, perhaps, of a poor man attempting to take a moral stance against an upper-class rake. Sostratos rides this tide by a declaration of honorable intention. He has fallen in love with the girl and wants to propose marriage. Gorgias immediately climbs down from his high horse so far as to declare himself pacified, although he warns Sostratos that his is a lost cause:

GORGIAS: So give up, my friend. You're on a loser. For us it's different. He's the penance Fate demands of family.

SOSTRATOS: But love. Have you never been in love, a young man like you?

GORGIAS: Hardly.

SOSTRATOS: Whyever not? What's to stop you?

GORGIAS: Economics, that's what. We can't afford luxuries. (338–44)

Several of the play's main issues are raised here: the gap in lifestyle between rich and poor; the imperative of blood ties; the sense of love being a one-sided affliction, the only result being a male-inspired relationship whose stability is the result of social status. One part of Gorgias is sympathetic to the prospect of his half-sister finding a rich husband: the other half of Gorgias cannnot resist making Sostratos aware of how the other half live. Gorgias' slave Daos is quite happy to get a day's digging out of a total stranger. Gorgias has the more solid purpose of testing the young man's resolve.

By the time they next appear together, Gorgias and Sostratos seem to have become firm friends. Sostratos is inviting Gorgias to the family feast and in no time at all will be suggesting that he marry his sister. It is at this point, the beginning of Act Four, that Knemon falls down the well and Gorgias, with minimal help from Sostratos and none at all from anyone else, manages to rescue him. The ensuing scene is a fascinating one. It is Gorgias' instinctive sympathy that provokes Knemon's *apologia*. That in turn makes of Knemon for the audience a more understandable character as he adopts Gorgias and gives him authority to conduct his affairs. Gorgias, who opens as a decent but ineffectual man, gains authority, position, and marriage into a wealthy family. Virtue, the very virtue that Knemon refuses to admit still exists, is rewarded by the tangible marks of success. It may be too late for Knemon to change his spots, but Gorgias confounds his basic thesis about the world's corruption.

Gorgias, then, and Knemon balance one another as fully fledged characters in a stage world where only selected characters have no off-stage existence. This limitation extends to all the professionals, the slaves—however ingenious—and, as a class, women. The women in Menander's comedies present a sticking-point for any modern audience. So much is it a man's world, as we have seen, that female characters sometimes have no name but are referred to simply as the Daughter or the Wife. The expectations of women at this time were severely limited.[6] An Athenian daughter would have marriage arranged for her by her father. The same, however, was true as often as not for a son. The options for non-Athenian women were far worse. They were excluded from all professions except the oldest, from which they might be plucked, as Chrysis in *The Woman from Samos*, to be the exclusive property of a man of substance. The expulsion scene in *The Woman from Samos* shows how precarious that status might prove.[7]

Theophrastus did write a treatise on marriage, cataloguing the various vices in women which should give a man pause. Among these vices are extravagance and shrewishness and, a little surprisingly, infidelity. Unfaithful wives have no place in the dramatic repertoire of New Comedy although the suspicion of unfaithfulness reduces the "wronged" male to reprehensible states of callousness. Any advantages marriage might offer can, in the opinion of Theophrastus, be accommodated in other ways. It will always be a pig in a poke.

> There's no choice with a wife; we have to keep her of whatever kind she is. If she is bad-tempered, stupid, ugly, proud, unpleasant, whatever her defects, we learn them after marriage. A horse, ass, ox, dog, the cheapest slaves, clothes and kettles, seats, cups, jugs of earthenware are examined before they are bought; only a wife is not on show for fear she should displease before her marriage.[8]

This thought appears to be echoed, as Webster points out, in a fragment of Menander in which an unidentified character says: "We ought to use the same care in marriage as in buying . . . we never examine or see the character of a wife with whom we are to live."[9] Menander, however, was adept at fitting sentiments to character. Such a remark in the mouth of an irascible old man such as the Nikeratos of *The Woman from Samos* or even the Knemon of *The Malcontent* is no more a reflection on the attitudes of the playwright than are Nikeratos' complaints about the Black Sea or Knemon's about the whole state of humankind.

Nevertheless, there is no escaping the fact that Menander did reflect an era when a male perspective was the only one available. The theatre was still a male province, as was every other facet of public life. Playwrights were men. Actors were men. If women appeared at all on stage in the plays of Aristophanes, it was as dancing girls whose only function was to be ogled at. Three of Aristophanes' plays might seem to imply a more significant influence for women within Athens but appearances are deceptive.

Festival Time (Thesmophoriazousai) is set in and about the festival of the Thesmophoria, a festival exclusive to women, but manages to contain no female character of consequence. Instead, it concentrates on Euripides and his attempts to infiltrate the festival. *Lysistrata*, celebrated in Britain for having so long been refused a license in the time of the censorship of plays by the office of the Lord Chamberlain, is less a sex comedy than a comedy about men's sexual appetite. As the only way to force peace on a warlike male population, the women of Athens resolve to deny sex to their men as long as the war lasts. Bawdy as the outcome is, the play is very much a "drag" play, the role of Lysistrata written with a male actor in mind. *Women in Power (Ekklesiazousai)* employs and doubles up on "drag" jokes when the women of Athens (played by male actors) enter at the beginning of the play, disguised as their husbands in order that they may go to the Assembly and vote women into power. The joke is extended in the next scene when the husbands arrive, dressed in their wives' clothes, having got out of bed and been unable to find their own. Such bluff and double bluff may be comic enough, but even when the women do take over, the resulting satire is never directed at the assumptions of society but turns into a loose consideration of Platonic ideas about shared property.

If Aristophanes notably reinforced the expectations of his male audiences, Euripides could at least be said to have challenged some of them. Of his nineteen plays, eight take their title from a female character and three others from the female chorus. His women range from the self-sacrificing and rather shadowy Alkestis, who chooses to die in her husband's place, to the vengeful Phaedra who, rejected by her stepson Hippolytus, kills herself, leaving a vindictive letter claiming he tried to rape her. Yet Hippolytus' own callousness and a private squabble between the goddesses Artemis and Aphrodite make their contribution to the tragedy.

In play after play, Euripides appears to demonstrate sympathy for women and the positions into which they are forced. His Klytemnestra in *Elektra* and *Iphigeneia in Aulis* are portrayals as sympathetic as the given circumstances will allow.[10] The three Helens of *Trojan Women*, *Helen*, and *Orestes* are highly individualized, the eponymous one a chaste and resourceful wife who never went to Troy at all.

The only curiosity in all this is Euripides' reputation as a misogynist. In Aristophanes' *Festival Time*, Euripides, as a stage character, wants to send someone to the all-woman festival because he has heard that the women of Athens intend to condemn him to death for the evil light in which he portrays them in his plays. The accusation recurs in *Frogs* where Euripides again appears as one of the cast, this time engaged in a battle with an equally fictional Aeschylus over who is the better playwright. One of Aeschylus' accusations against his rival is that his introduction of women like Phaedra and Sthenoboea into his plays was so shaming that decent women went home and poisoned themselves. Euripides' defense is not to point to the number of sympathetic roles he initiated but to suggest that, if such women exist, he ought to write about them.

The belief that the Athenian playwrights were incapable of seeing a woman's point of view is not borne out by the plays we have. Euripides might be regarded as a special case, but consider the plea of Deianira, wife of Herakles, in Sophocles' often overlooked *Women of Trachis*:

> It will not take my dying
> To recognise my life as ill-starred, full of grief.
> When I was still in my father Oeneus' house

> I first acquired a desperate fear of sex
> Worse than any unmarried girl in Aetolia.

She proceeds to relate how Herakles fought for her hand:

> I cowered there, paralysed with fear,
> The fear that beauty like mine can only lead to misery.
> Zeus decreed that the fight should end happily.
> Happily, I suppose. But since I've been Herakles' wife
> I've worried about him ceaselessly, night and day,
> Fear breeds fear. Night follows lonely night,
> Dispelling some fears, creating others, worse.
> We've had a family but he sees them no more often
> Than a farmer visits his boundary field.
> (*Women of Trachis* 4–7 and 24–32)[11]

Menander, as we have seen, has recourse more often to the tragic or tragicomic worlds of Sophocles or Euripides than to the slapstick farrago of Aristophanic Old Comedy, where women may never receive sensitive treatment. Nor do men as they badger and bully their way through a series of fantastical situations. A play such as Menander's *The Arbitration*, with rape apparently condoned when it transpires that the rapist has unwittingly married the victim, is an archetypal example of the male orientation of New Comedy. It may be, however, that there are indications, if only sporadic, that Menander's worldview was sufficiently sympathetic to pay some attention to the condition of all his characters, while concentrating only on some of them.

Although *The Arbitration* is barely half complete, the outline of the plot is clear enough. When Charisios discovers that his wife has given birth only five months after their marriage, he moves out to live next door and invites in a music-girl Habrotonon. His alternative would have been to hand Pamphile back to her father, along with her dowry; why he chooses not to take this course of action is unclear. Her father, another Smikrines, seems more concerned about the cost of the whore than any insult to his daughter.

Clearly, the morality of such a tale is at best uncomfortable, particularly as the rapist who fathered Pamphile's child turns out to have been Charisios anyway. Pamphile's distress over the rape; the pregnancy; the hastily arranged marriage, with its accompanying duplicity; the scorn of her husband and his desertion; the birth of the child; its exposure, the assumption being that it will not survive; Pamphile's subsequent humiliation; the final revelation that her husband is a rapist—none of this is exactly comic. What it is is "given." The audience is not invited to comment on past events or to speculate too much on this occasion about the eventual prospects for the marriage once all is sorted out. Menander's plot outlines are apparently conventional in that they cover a similar limited range to those of his contemporaries, the same as are picked up a hundred years later in their own adaptations by Plautus and Terence. Much of Renaissance comedy is as guilty of offering the untenable sentiment and situation. Claudio's rejection of Hero at the wedding ceremony in *Much Ado About Nothing* leaves a sour taste in the mouth which the unmasking of Don John cannot entirely remove, while *The Taming of the Shrew* has become almost unplayable.

What preserves Shakespeare and what raised Menander above his contemporaries and his imitators was the manner in which they handled scenes, not the plot lines they employed. The revelation to Pamphile in *The Arbitration* that the baby is still alive and that Charisios is the father is not dealt with in a perfunctory manner. It is Habrotonon, the woman with whom Charisios is trying to console himself, who tells her the truth and with no ulterior motive. Both here and in the scene where her father suggests that she move back to his house, Pamphile behaves with dignity and charity. No sooner has Habrotonon told her what really happened than Charisios' slave Onesimos emerges to describe how Charisios has reacted:

> There was no stopping him. "What a wife I married and what a mess I've made of things." Then when he had heard everything, he rushed off indoors, groaning, tearing his hair, out of his mind. "Look at me. What a swine I am. I do something like that and father a bastard child: and then show no feeling at all, have not a moment's sympathy for a woman who found herself in such a situation." (889–97)

If this were some token remorse, reported at second hand, that might be it, but Charisios then enters himself and pours more recrimination on his own head. The point is that at this stage he does not know that the woman he raped is now his wife and that the baby is his. His remorse is due entirely to his having faced up to his dual standard of blaming his wife for having an illegitimate child at the same time as knowing that he himself had forced his attentions on an unwilling victim. The morality may still be difficult to stomach but with the plot prescribed, the reactions could hardly be more heartfelt.

A woman's right to have a say in her own destiny is seldom an issue in a society that saw so few alternatives between being a wife and being a whore. *The Man She Hated* (*Misoumenos*) appears to be remarkable in this, though so little survives that nothing should be taken as finalized. It appears from the surviving fragments, and the title bears this out, to be about a soldier who has captured a girl in war but who then finds her refusing to sleep with him. In a position to compel her into his bed, he declines to do so and spends much of the play speculating on why she has rejected him. The fact that she might simply not wish to go to bed with him is an explanation that does not seem to have occurred to those critics who have written about the play. If Menander sees material in this apparently slight idea for an entire comedy, there were no doubt refinements and complications. What is interesting is the premise. On this occasion, it is not assumed that if a man takes a fancy to a girl he has the automatic right to expect her to feel the same way about him. Krateia does not feel like that about Thrasonides, although the outcome would appear to be that she is ransomed by her father and by choice agrees to marry the man she has spent the play rejecting. The conceit of the male characters can sometimes be breathtaking, but it is frequently put into a context where the playwright does not condone the attitude of his character.

The Malcontent does not have a major female role. Love story though the Prologue declares it, this is a supremely one-sided affair. Sostratos, with a little bit of help from Pan, has fallen in love at first sight with Knemon's unnamed daughter. He happens to be present when she comes from her house to lament over the loss of the bucket which the Nurse has dropped down the well. Pan has already described her as "an innocent" who "hasn't a mean thought in her head." That is about the extent of her personality, though her step-brother and even his slave feel especially protective toward her, as we later discover. Effectively, however, her anonymity says it all. There is no mileage in her as an individual, so she gets no opportunity to show that she might be one. This attitude is not confined to women in the plays. Each stage character in *The Malcontent* serves his or her dramatic purpose and no more. The more the play's theme is concentrated on a single issue or a single relationship, the more the peripherals hide behind a stock-in-trade: in *The Malcontent* being the object of infatuation is stock-in-trade enough.

The other female characters are as functional. The old woman Simiche is necessary to let everyone know what is happening indoors: otherwise the daughter would have to keep coming in and out, and that would contravene social convention. Rather more interesting is Myrrhine, the widow whom Knemon once married but who left him, an option open in Greece to any wife who could manage to support herself without her husband. She appears late in the play, after Knemon's accident. Her immediate reaction is one of sympathy. She offers to look after him in her house. She and her son Gorgias are on the receiving end of Knemon's long and enlightening speech where he justifies his approach to life. Knemon seems to reject any chance of a reconciliation with Myrrhine, but seeing her and her son in such a kindly light does reveal how much Knemon turns his back on when he opts for solitude. Sostratos' mother and sister also put in an appearance but simply to set up the circumstance of the family party and to show the girl whose hand is later to be offered to Gorgias. To develop any of these further would be to add a layer of complexity the play does not need.

If *The Malcontent* has little to add to Menander's possible concern for women, *The Woman from Samos* is much more informative. Nikeratos' daughter, Plangon—the name means "doll"—puts in no more than a token appearance. There is no opportunity for her to tell what she thinks of Moschion who seduced her and whose child she has now borne. Considering how often rape by unknown assailants features as the trigger to a stage plot, a confessed seduction is a positive rarity, as, indeed, it probably was in real life when young women lived such secluded lives. There is at least a chance that this relationship could be a mutual love affair that requires only the sanction of paternal approval. Moschion's reticence to admit what happened is in keeping both with his character and with his upbringing.

Similarly, Nikeratos' wife has no lines and makes one notional entrance at the end of the play. Nevertheless, she is a formidable off-stage presence, being privy to all the machinations and all the deceptions relating to both households. When Nikeratos returns in Act Two after going to tell his family that he has arranged for Plangon to get married, the text is defective, but he clearly was given a dusty reception. It seems that what he forgot to mention to his wife and daughter was that Moschion was to be the bridegroom. Circumstances being as they are, the women are unenthusiastic. "He won't find it easy convincing his wife, that's for sure," says Demeas to Nikeratos' retreating back. "You should never waste time explaining things to people" (200–202).

Act Four opens with Nikeratos' entrance as he talks back to his wife who is still indoors. His instinctive defense of Chrysis and the offer of protection in his house have clearly not been enough for Myrrhine who now expects him to tackle Demeas directly: "Woman, you'll be the death of me. I'll go and see him this minute" (421). What is unusual in *The Woman from Samos* is the powerful sense of a complete off-stage family life. When Demeas relates how he overheard the conversation that has led him to believe the baby belongs to Chrysis and that Moschion is the father, the speech conjures up a wonderful picture of a rich man's household in turmoil from wedding preparations. The plays of New Comedy take place in public, and that is where the men are at their most influential. *The Woman from Samos* shows us the domestic interior where women's rule holds sway.

Chrysis, the Samian herself, is a major study. Secure enough of her hold over Demeas, she can initiate the temporary deception: "Father's going to be so angry," declares the apprehensive Moschion. "And after a while," she replies serenely, "he'll stop being angry. Because, my dear, he loves me. He's in love and he can't help himself, any more than you can. 'Love hath the better of temper.' Besides I'd put up with anything rather than see the poor mite in some slum foster-home" (79–85).

Chrysis gives every impression of being a cultivated and intelligent woman whose expulsion from Samos has left her no alternative but to exercise the profession of courtesan.[12] Demeas' initial resistance to inviting her into his home was, we discover, broken down by his son. Chrysis herself had no objections. "Presumably," wrote T.B.L. Webster, "security and probably the hope of a legacy persuaded Chrysis to give up the ten drachmai or more that she has been earning per night on her own."[13] This is a remarkably thick-skinned response to both character and situation. Chrysis is not only the kindest person in the play; she is also the cleverest.

When the play was known mainly from fragments and before the last act was discovered, critics usually assumed that the end must have included the discovery that Chrysis was all along a citizen, perhaps even Moschion's sister, who could therefore legally marry Demeas. As we now know, she is edged out of the final scenes except as a witness to the marriage of Moschion and the daughter. This marginalizing is of a piece with how other characters treat her throughout the play. Her rejection by Demeas when he believes she has had a child by Moschion is a complete surprise to her because Demeas refuses to put his suspicions into words. This is a painful scene because of her belief that she could predict Demeas' behavior.

Chrysis' subsequent rejection by Nikeratos, by which time Demeas has discovered the real truth, is blatantly comic, with Chrysis having to save the baby after Nikeratos goes berserk. Her escape onto the stage from Nikeratos' house, only to be welcomed back into Demeas' house, reaches a point of pure farce. By this juncture any personal threat to Chrysis is over, and she retires as far as the drama is concerned to the fringes of the action, allowing Menander to focus on the central relationship in the play, namely, father and adopted son. Nonetheless, a warm and sympathetic playing of the role can make Chrysis seem to be at the center of everything that happens. Webster believed that Demeas was the spine of *The Woman from Samos* in the same way as *The Malcontent* can be said to be "about" Knemon. A closer reading, confirmed in production, shows that the play revolves less around any one individual than around a family unit that will only function properly once Demeas and Moschion have learned how to be honest with one another.

The solution to the father and son relationship in *The Woman from Samos* comes in the unexpected last act. Here, for what seems to be the first time, Demeas and Moschion talk frankly to one another. Their motives for not doing so elsewhere are honorable enough, but what betrays them is a lack of trust. When the play opens Moschion confides in the audience "the sort of man my father is." Moschion is an adopted son and this appears to have placed a certain stress on their relationship, a stress of obligation on the one side and the need to offer only the best example on the other.

The liaison between Demeas and Chrysis is at one level no more than a means of putting Moschion's affair into perspective. Although nothing in Athenian life would suggest that a bachelor were behaving improperly by sharing his house with a "professional" mistress, Demeas declined to commit himself for fear of setting Moschion a bad example. He only agreed to take her into his house on the condition that there must be no children.

Moschion's fear of his father's reaction to his indiscretion is rooted in his determination not to let Demeas down. Though something of a feckless individual, incapable of making any decision on his own, Moschion is afraid less of his father's anger than of his disapproval. Hence Chrysis risks her neck by pretending that the baby is hers, even though she has been expressly forbidden to keep her child. Demeas' reason for that may well be a fear of Chrysis appearing to claim the status of a wife and hence interfere with his relationship with Moschion. Demeas proves to be a forceful man but for the most part affable. It is he who has suggested to Nikeratos that Moschion should marry Plangon, even though he knows that his neighbor cannot afford a dowry. It is, he assumes, his right to pick a wife for his son, but a son's wishes are more respected in this than ever a daughter's might be.

Demeas and Moschion's first meeting is overshadowed by both of them being apprehensive about getting around to the main subject on their minds. The fact that the subject is the same for both of them, marriage, and so is the object, Plangon, gives a nice edge. Moschion turns out to be less feeble on other people's account than he is on his own, an unexpected touch. When Demeas later threatens to turn Chrysis out, Moschion leaps to argue the point in the fascinating exchange already quoted in a different context in Chapter 1:

DEMEAS: What do you expect me to do? Bring up a child that's illegitimate? Not my style. Oh no, not my style at all.

MOSCHION: Illegitimate? Who's legitimate, for god's sake? Any man born might
be illegitimate.

DEMEAS: It's just a joke to you, isn't it?

MOSCHION: I'm perfectly serious, I swear it. I can see no distinction between
being of one race or another. To anyone who believes in justice, if a man's
good, he's legitimate and if he's bad, he's a bastard. (135–43)

Admittedly, Moschion has an oblique interest in the outcome of such a
debate, but the exchange does set him up, not merely as the foolish young
man to whom we have been initially introduced, but as someone capable of
taking his father on over a moral issue. The loss of nearly thirty lines
immediately after the above exchange is especially disappointing, for, in
the course of them, Demeas gets around to suggesting that Moschion marry
Plangon and Moschion admits that this is what he had in mind himself. That,
of course, was the moment to confess that he has somewhat jumped the gun:
but if he did the play would end in Act Two.

In his pleasure at sorting out the wedding, Demeas, whose anger can be
ferocious but is quickly dissipated, appears to reconcile himself to Chrysis'
child.[14] The bombshell occurs when he overhears a nurse identifying a baby
as being Moschion's and immediately spies it being breastfed by Chrysis.
The ensuing turmoil is the result of a double deception with Parmenon
caught in the middle, not knowing what he dare admit to whom. All is
compounded by Demeas' insistence that he knows everything that is going
on, when all that he knows is half of it. According to plan, Parmenon tells
Demeas that Chrysis is the baby's mother. When Demeas forces him to
confess that Moschion is the father, Parmenon omits to modify his former
story and confess that it is Plangon, not Chrysis, who is the baby's mother.

Demeas' anguish is real enough. He assumes from Moschion's reactions to
the proposed marriage that all the blame for what has happened must be laid
at Chrysis' door. Grossly unjust as this may be, it is the only interpretation that
Demeas, who knows and loves his son, can place on the facts as he sees them:

I still can't fathom how a lad who seemed so restrained and so reasonable
with everyone else could treat his father like this. I don't care if he was
adopted ten times over, natural son or not, it's character that counts. I look to
nothing else. The woman's a whore, an infection. (343–48)

To give Demeas his due, he does not find it as easy as that:

Be a man, Demeas. Govern your passions. Fall out of love. And as far as
possible, hush up the whole business. For Moschion's sake. Pitch her out of

the house. Oh my lovely Samian girl. To hell with her. You've got your
excuse. She wouldn't get rid of the baby. That's all anyone need to know.
(349–55)

The sheer cruelty of the next scene has been understated in some
translations. As it stands, Demeas appears vindictive and cowardly, particularly as he declines to explain to Chrysis why he is rejecting her. His
determination to keep up appearances and a refusal to put anything unpleas-
ant into words are keynotes to the man's character as well as being a valuable
plot device. Moschion's spirited defense of Chrysis is again based on the
two men's refusal to talk directly:

DEMEAS: Moschion. Will you allow me? Allow me, Moschion. And for the third
    time. I know everything.
MOSCHION: Everything about what?
DEMEAS: I don't want to discuss it. (465–66)

Nikeratos' presence makes things worse as he begins to cotton on to what
Demeas thinks has happened. Nikeratos has no qualms about putting things
into words:

NIKERATOS: What an unmitigated catastrophe.
DEMEAS: It's me who's been wronged, you know, but at least I kept it to myself.
NIKERATOS: You've a slave mentality, Demeas. If it was my nest he'd fouled,
    he'd never have done it a second time, and nor would his mate. If it had been
    a tart of mine, I'd have sold her off tomorrow and disinherited my son while
    I was at it. It'd have been the talk of the town in every barber's shop and every
    arcade. From dawn to dusk everybody would have been saying what a fine
    fellow Nikeratos was, putting his son on a murder charge.
MOSCHION: Murder charge?
NIKERATOS: I'd call it murder if someone treated me like that. (505–14)

When Nikeratos leaves, Moschion finally brings himself to confess to
Demeas what really happened. Demeas is then faced with further hood-
winking Nikeratos with a cock and bull story about Zeus being the likely
father of Plangon's baby. Nikeratos sees through it, but by this time his fury
too has subsided: "Damn me if it isn't Moschion making me look an idiot"
(597). All is explained and apparently forgiven. The wedding can now take
place, and Chrysis is restored to the affections and household of Demeas:
except for one thing—there is still a whole act to go.

Act Five opens with Moschion who, having had some time to consider what has happened, is furious that his father could have suspected him of being involved with Chrysis. If he could muster up the nerve he would leave home to join the army, but, as he could not face it, he decides he must pretend to in order to teach Demeas a lesson. Put-upon slave Parmenon, after a classic speech in which he absolves himself from responsibility for what has happened, attempts to dissuade Moschion from leaving and sets up the final scene in which Moschion confronts his father. Demeas' apology for jumping to the wrong conclusion is heartfelt and warm. The manner in which he dismissed Chrysis from his house may have been shocking, but there is little arguing with David Bain's verdict that "*Samia* is par excellence a play about basically 'nice' people."[15]

DEMEAS: Oh Moschion. You're upset and I love you for it. I can't say I blame
   you when I made such a groundless accusation against you. I was wrong. All
   I can do is ask you to consider this. Even in bad times, I'm still your father.
   I took you in when you were a baby and I've brought you up. If your life has
   had some joy in it, give me credit for that and balance it against the pain I've
   caused, as a son should. I blamed you for something you never did. That was
   unfair. I shouldn't have done it. I must have been out of my mind. That's the
   way of it. I was trying to protect your reputation in the eyes of the world, so
   I confided in no one. And all along I was holding the wrong end of the stick.
   (694–705)

This gracious speech acknowledges a fault and accounts for it in a way that implies that Demeas will have learned for the future, both to worry less about what other people think and to speak out on matters that trouble him instead of letting misunderstandings develop from *agnoia*, the goddess of ignorance.

But Demeas has not yet finished. He has a word of correction for his son:

But I never said a word that an enemy could gloat over. What you're doing
is broadcasting this mistake of mine and telling the world what a fool I've
been. That's not worthy of you, Moschion. Don't allow the one day in your
life when I let you down drive out the memory of the past. There's more I
could say but, never mind. Grudging obedience won't do, you know. A father
needs respect. (706–12)

At this moment Nikeratos, who had advocated spreading Moschion's shame to the skies, enters to tell them to get a move on because everything's ready for the wedding. Nikeratos' blustering threats persuade Moschion that he has won his point, although Moschion makes sure he has the last word:

"If you'd behaved like this in the first place, Father, we could have done without the moralising" (724–25).

And so the play ends with a greater understanding between Demeas and Moschion as a result of all that has happened. The way in which Menander chooses to sideline all but his two leading characters can be alarming, but with a speaking cast of only six, the dramatic method is easier to pin down than in *The Malcontent*, for example, where the wood sometimes obscures the trees.

Such a detailed analysis of a single relationship needs no apology because, in any final analysis, it is what *The Woman from Samos* is about. How Menander's method, both here and elsewhere may have changed the face of subsequent drama must, of course, be a speculative study because so few dramatists of subsequent generations had the opportunity to study his work. The Romans did know him as a living playwright, and it is through this extension of New Comedy that we may be able to posit some broader areas of stage technique to which Menander can, perhaps, be said to have given birth.

NOTES

1. For the full text, see *Appendix 1*.
2. F. H. Sandbach, *Manipulation of Language* in *Ménandre*, Vol. XVI, Vandoevres-Genève. Fondation-Hardt, 1969, pp. 113–14.
3. Aristotle, *Poetics*, Ch. VI.
4. Theophrastus, *Characters*, X.
5. W. G. Arnott, *Menander I*, Cambridge, Mass. and London: Heinemann and Harvard University Press, 1979, pp. 90–91.
6. There have been a number of valuable recent studies of the position of women in Athenian society, among them W. K. Lacey, *The Family in Classical Greece*, London: Thames and Hudson, 1968 and R. Just, *Women in Athenian Law and Life*, London and New York: Routledge, 1989.
7. See M. M. Henry, *Menander's Courtesans and the Greek Comic Tradition*, Frankfurt and New York: Lang, 1985, Chapter 4.
8. As quoted by T.B.L. Webster in *Studies in Menander*, 2nd ed., Manchester: Manchester University Press, 1960, p. 215.
9. Fragment 581.
10. The French director Ariane Mnouchkine chose to open her production of Aeschylus' *Oresteia* with Euripides' *Iphigeneia in Aulis* in order to account for Klytemnestra's hostility to Agamemnon.
11. Translation as in *Sophocles Plays: Two*, London: Methuen, 1990.
12. Her position is considered in context in E. Fantham, "Sex, Status and Survival in Hellenistic Athens: A Study of Women in New Comedy" in *Phoenix*, Vol. 29, 1975, pp. 65–66.

13. T.B.L. Webster, *Introduction to Menander*, Manchester: Manchester University Press, 1974, p. 30.

14. See the Methuen translation for my solution to the scene.

15. Menander, *Samia*, Warminster: Aris and Phillips, 1983, p. xviii.

Chapter 6

Menander's Legacy

The first person to have written a book of theatre history was probably Juba, king of Numidia, whose other claim to fame was, suitably enough, to have been the son-in-law of Antony and Cleopatra. Born some two hundred and fifty years after the death of Menander and the best part of five hundred years after the birth of Aeschylus, he would have had to delve deep to find any coherent pattern in the history of the art form which, above all others, is characterized by impermanence. What he must have had access to were far more plays by the great playwrights than have survived to the twentieth century and a wealth of incidental comment on theatre conditions that had begun to emerge piecemeal from the fourth century onward.

The revelations that such a volume might have contained are too tantalizing a prospect to dwell upon, but it is not unreasonable to conjecture that one of Juba's starting points in his research might have been Aristotle's parallel works on tragedy and comedy. The work on tragedy, known as the *Poetics*, survives: the work on comedy does not and remains today most celebrated as a source for fictional speculation in Umberto Eco's *The Name of the Rose*.

Both of Aristotle's works were celebrated in his own time, and it would be a surprise if Menander had not been familiar with both. Whether the work on comedy taught him anything about his craft we shall never know. The *Poetics*, if a flawed document which Juba might have found created more problems than it solved about the origins of tragedy and comedy, still offers insights into the process of playwriting. In the Renaissance, and for centuries after, Aristotle was assumed to have created a set of rules for dramatic composition, when what he was doing was little more than observing the process as he had found it. So, while he mentions a division into acts and interludes, observed by the playwrights of his own and earlier times through the *entr'actes* from the chorus, his passing comments about the unities of time and place are far from prescriptive. None of the surviving fifth-century playwrights of tragedy seem to have concerned themselves with completing the action of a play within a single day or confining themselves to a single location. Both often happen: neither is a rule. As for Aristophanes, his plays have a wholly anarchic sense of time and place which is part of their charm.

It is still true that in all the Menander plays we know of, including the fragmentary majority, the structure is simple enough to require neither change of location nor an extended timescale beyond the events of a single day. Progress through the day from dawn till dusk may have seemed the only natural time sequence if the tenets of realism were not to be violated. Since the location is customarily identified in the opening speech, the action needs no enhancement from a set-change.

Aristotle does pin down two of the fundamental features of dramatic structure that are as pertinent for the comedies of Menander as they are for the classical tragedies at which they were aimed, namely, *peripeteia* and *anagnorisis*. *Peripeteia* is a reversal of fortune or expectation; *anagnorisis* is the recognition, either of a lost baby/parent/trinket, or, less directly, of a truth, a revelation that sorts everything out and heads the audience and the characters for home. The analysis already made of *The Malcontent* and *The Woman from Samos*, as well as the various sequences from *The Arbitration*, *The Shield*, and *The Shorn Girl*, demonstrate less that Menander wrote his plays according to any Aristotelian formula than that Aristotle did pin down and identify two of the fundamentals of dramatic technique. If his revelations seem at this distance to look like little more than common sense, perhaps it is the result of a further two thousand years of absorption by anyone who ever set out to write a piece for the stage.

To some extent the same is true of any search for the influence that Menander may have had on the future writing of comedy within the Western dramatic tradition. It is no trifling question to ask how Menander could be said to have had any influence at all on comic form from medieval times onward when until 1957 no one had the opportunity to study any of his plays: not unless his techniques have survived in some dramatic racial memory, enabling later generations to follow his lead subliminally just as, psychologists tell us, the discovery of how to balance on two wheels in the nineteenth-century made it easier for twentieth-century children not to fall off their bicycles.

Fortunately, we are saved from such dubious delvings into the psyche for two reasons. The first is that Menander, as we now know, did open a seam so rich it shows no sign of running out. If anything, television has given it a new lease of life. One British situation comedy, "One Foot in the Grave," has won plaudits and awards by resurrecting a latter-day Knemon, a man so disenchanted with the world that the world manages constantly to reinforce his every prejudice.

The second link is that of Roman New Comedy. Plautus and Terence may not be proper substitutes for Menander, but they did Latinize Menander and his contemporaries for a new age. Plautus is less influential here but as recently as 1968 E. W. Handley was able to reveal a passage of some fifty lines from Menander's *Double Deceiver* (*Dis Exapaton*), which overlaps with a Plautine adaptation, *The Two Bacchises*.[1] The Menander is part of two acts, split by a chorus. Such divisions had disappeared entirely in Roman comedy, and the Plautus is a continuous sequence. Dialogue in Plautus is diminished in favor of a long speech (perhaps sung), but the main difference is located, as Norma Miller points out in her Penguin translation which contains both passages, in tone: "Plautus is broader, more emphatic and elaborate in his comedy and comic effects, playing for a laugh rather than an appreciative smile."[2]

The vogue for adapting Greek New Comedy gave a serious, or at least literary, comic dimension to a Roman theatre that had its own indigenous aspects, both tragic and comic, but was negligible by comparison with the Greek classics. The process of adaptation was known as *contaminatio*, a term used confusingly both as a guarantee of quality and as an accusation of plagiarism. It is difficult to imagine a theatre so dominated by works from the past, but since the 1980s Tom Stoppard has in a similar way revivified nineteenth-century Viennese classics with dazzling adaptations of Nestroy, Molnar, and Schnitzler.[3]

The extent of most Roman adaptations is not easy to decipher, though it is pretty clear that Plautus brought a more ribald and brash quality to his originals than did Terence, a writer whose style, as Stoppard's, has the precision and fascination for wordplay of someone who is not writing in the language he first learned. Publius Terentius Afer, to give him the full name he acquired when freed by his master Terentius Lucanus, was an African brought to Rome as a slave. His talent gave him access to artistic circles and to the public theatre, though not always without acrimony as his prologues bear witness.

One play of Terence does provide a real point of comparison to Menander over a question relating to the generation gap. Greek comedy offered a perennial debate over the way in which children should be brought up. Terence's *Brothers* (*Adelphi*) is based on a play of the same name by Menander, with one scene from Diphilus. A piece of considerable sensitivity, *Brothers* contains at its core a serious parable of the balance between nature and nurture. Two brothers, Aeschinus and Ctesipho, have been brought up, for reasons that need not detain us, one by the real father Demea and the other by Demea's brother and uncle to the boys, Micio. The play is largely a study in temperaments. Demea is strict, Micio lax. Demea is appalled at the license offered to Aeschinus, even though he has legally disclaimed responsibility for him.

The abducting of a slave girl from her master by Aeschinus provokes the plot. Aeschinus is about to settle down and is due to get married. The abduction, and the consequent seeing off of the girl's pimp, are effected on behalf of the younger brother who is in the process of breaking the shackles but is terrified of his father finding out. The complications multiply until all is revealed and sorted out. The sting in the tail is that the puritan Demea decides to abandon all his previous standards as license appears to be the only way to curry favor with the young. He authorizes the breaking down of the division between Micio's house and the one next door, wins his brother's slaves their freedom, and foists a wife onto the confirmed bachelor Micio. The reversal is wonderfully managed.

Micio's initial stance is sympathetic:

> If fear of punishment is all that guarantees good
> behaviour in a man, oh he'll behave, as long as someone is
> watching. But he'll bide his time until he can get away
> with it and revert. . . . It's the same with being a father.
> Get a son in the habit of doing the right thing and not
> just because he's frightened of you. That's the difference
> between a father and an autocrat. If anyone doesn't agree,
> he should confess that he hasn't the first idea about
> bringing up children. (*Brothers* 69–77)

For much of *Brothers*, all the sympathy seems to be with the liberal Micio, although an eyebrow or two may be raised at the behavior he condones. In the last act, when the immediate problems are solved, the debate on upbringing is resumed. Micio points to both the boys and claims them as decent young men "full of common sense, intelligence, caution when it's called for and mutual affection" (827–28). His argument seems unassailable. Demea responds by showing that such freedom is just a way of buying goodwill: and he demonstrates his thesis to the intense frustration of his brother:

MICIO: What's going on, Demea? How come the transformation? What's got into you? Why the fit of generosity?

DEMEA: I'll tell you. So that I can demonstrate something to you. People may find you good-natured and cheerful, Micio, but that doesn't mean you live a decent life. It doesn't mean that what you do is fair or correct. It simply shows what you can buy by being complacent, permissive and extravagant. I put it to you, Aeschinus. If you and your brother reject my way of life because I am not prepared to overturn basic decencies, then I reject you. Waste money. Spend all you like. Do what the devil you want. If, on the other hand, you would prefer someone available to offer you advice when a young man's appetite overrules his discretion; if you want someone to restrain you and tell you when you make a mistake; if you need someone who will always be there when you need him, here I am. I'll be your man. (984–95)

Aeschinus submits, and the play ends within half a dozen lines.

Whether such moralizing, of the sort that made Terence so popular in late medieval times, is the product of Roman *gravitas* or a faithful rendition of his source cannot be known. The fifth act change of direction in *Brothers* is certainly a Menandrian trait that Terence inherits, and the sentiments are not so far from what Menander might be expected to have written. The collision between alternative philosophies of education is less subtle than the exploration in *The Woman from Samos* of the relationship between adoptive father and adopted son, but there is a similar hint that the defect that makes them so reticent with one another is the strength of their desire to please. This is a facet of character that demands subtlety and would hardly be appropriate at all in farce.

Plautus and Terence provide at this juncture an invaluable yardstick for the two directions in which so much later comedy has developed. Plautus, the marketplace champion, links up with the true street tradition and what Arnott earlier described as "the straw-hat circuit."[4] The *fabula Atellana*, a localized farce tradition from the Naples area which gave Plautus his early acting experience, was a flexible and part-improvised form that relied heavily on a set number of fixed characters who were catapulted into a whole series of new situations. The stock figures of the Atellan were Maccus, the fool;[5] Bucco, the braggart or glutton; Pappus, the foolish old man; and Dossennus, the wily one. Although it was the middle of the sixteenth century before *commedia dell' arte* surfaced as an independent dramatic form, some of the characters of the *commedia* again have local connections to Naples.

The surge of popularity of the improvised comedy, with its stock figures of Arlecchino, Pantalone, its lovers and its zanni, provided a repertoire of character types who were to become the basis of English pantomime and inspired writers and practitioners, up to and including our own century, as diverse as Molière and Stravinsky, Gozzi and Meyerhold. Central to the tradition is the mask, which provides one link, however unconscious a link, between the Hellenistic theatre and the twentieth century.[6]

The extent to which an Italian performing tradition can appear to stretch back to the time of Menander is a full study in itself. Here again Wiles[7] offers guidance and common sense. The more deeply we inquire, the more does the legacy of Menander lie in precisely the opposite direction. Plautus could, and perhaps did, allow for unscripted intrusion, for physical stage business and for a kind of performing mobility that made him entirely suitable for the hurly-burly of Roman festival. Menander was a crafted practitioner who created complex plays for the Great Dionysia in the first instance. The occasion may have been less hallowed than in the time of Aeschylus, but the Theatre of Dionysus had not returned to its marketplace origins and was probably a deal more respectable than when Aristophanes' rivals were currying favor by throwing the audience fruit and nuts.

Hence, we have the sense of a parting of the ways between the theatres of the vibrant Plautus and the more sophisticated Terence—the former fitting itself up to survive the Roman Empire and the dark ages despite a text, the latter following Menander's more scholarly path into the school-rooms and monasteries.[8] True, there were to be overlaps, notably in the plays of Shakespeare and Molière. Menander's legacy, however, will be found, if anywhere, not in slapstick and buffoonery but in the contemplation of human foible.

Eclectic as any further Menander-spotting must be, some sort of apology has to be in order for making the next station along this route the one play of Shakespeare which is unequivocally based on a Plautus original. After spending the last two pages apparently downgrading Plautus from a literary tradition, suddenly to introduce *The Comedy of Errors* might seem positively perverse. The proper defense is that to be part of the marketplace tradition, Peter Brook's "rough theatre,"[9] is nothing demeaning but a proud boast. Shakespeare's skill was to take Plautus' *Menaechmi*, a piece of fairly rough theatre, and impart into it a dramatic style and shape that far exceeds its origins.

Plautus used the theme of twins obliquely in his *Amphitruo* where Zeus and Mercury use supernatural disguise to effect the seduction of Alcumena in the only extant New Comedy with mythological characters. *Menaechmi* offers a more conventional New Comedy plot set in the Greek city of Epidamnus. Twin brothers were parted in childhood. Now grown up, one lives in Epidamnus and the other has come to look for his identical brother. The number of scenes of confusion is limited in Plautus by the number of acquaintances of the "home" Menaechmus whom the playwright can contrive to meet the "away" Menaechmus. There are several subsidiary characters, including a deceived wife, a courtesan, a parasite, a cook, and a doctor. The play has a cast of ten and is lively enough. What the original Greek play was remains unknown, but there were at least six Greek New Comedies with "twins" in the title, as Arnott recorded in the Introduction to his translation.[10] One of these was Menander's *Girl Twins* (*Didumai*), and he also wrote several others whose titles could hint at a similar source of confusion. The only aspect of *Menaechmi* which is difficult to tolerate is the sheer stupidity of the brother who has come to a foreign place in search of someone who looks exactly like him and who proceeds to be mystified by everyone he meets, mistaking him for someone else. At least his is the minor role of the two, thus placing the play's emphasis on the homelife of the Menaechmus who lives in Epidamnus.

Shakespeare confounds the situation by reversing the point of view so that his "away" Antipholus is the more important character. In addition, he gives both brothers twin servants to multiply the potential for misunderstanding and sets the play in Ephesus, a known seat of witchcraft. Shakespeare's "away" Antipholus is all the time expecting weird things to happen and responds, as does Dromio his servant, by assuming that he is running the gauntlet of "sprites and goblins."

Plautus offers a harmless farce with little differentiation between the characters and little concern on their behalf. Menander, on the evidence of the plays we have, is more concerned with his characters so that an audience will laugh with them, not at them. Shakespeare is in this way more Menandrian, and the way in which he gives the play real urgency is by means of a Prologue. The Prologue in *The Comedy of Errors* has something of the feel of Menander's *The Shield* in that it proposes a potential tragedy and uses this to frame the play. *The Comedy of Errors* is set in an Ephesus at odds with Syracuse, so that any Syracusan merchant found in Ephesus and unable to pay a thousand marks is condemned to death. Aegeon has not come to trade but to look for both of his sons, the one lost in childhood and the other not seen since he set off to find his brother. The Duke, in recognition of his plight, offers him a day to find the money.

With this single device, Shakespeare imparts a seriousness to the whole play that too few productions acknowledge. Behind every scene is a sense of urgency as the deadline draws near. The fact that none of the characters except those in the first scene is aware of what is going on bestows on the audience a similar privilege to that afforded by a Menandrian Prologue and enables them to enjoy the ramifications of the plot without the confusion of those who are living through it. A difference here between Menander and Shakespeare is that Menander tends to use his Prologue to reassure an audience, to let them know that all will end happily and that a resolution is only scenes away. The freedom this gives him is in the twists and turns of the plot as they head toward a known outcome. It assumes, I would submit, a certain refinement on the part of an audience whom the playwright expects to appreciate his craft.

Shakespeare does use suspense and he does use surprise. An audience encountering *The Comedy of Errors* for the first time may predict that a way will be found to save Aegeon's life and that the twins will be reunited with one another as well as with their father. No god is needed to tell them that before the play starts. What they are less likely to predict is that part of the agency that brings about the restoration of the family is the discovery of the mother living in chaste seclusion in a nearby abbey.

What links *The Comedy of Errors* thematically with, for example, *The Malcontent*, while ruling out all but the obvious parallels with *Menaechmi* is the sense of divine purpose. Menander, through the medium of Chance, Ignorance, or Pan, often acts as a kind of guardian angel to his characters. Shakespeare implies that there is a divine shape to the affairs of men and women. All will be resolved when humans stop abusing time—the play is crammed with examples of how they do so—and allow the restoration of the family unit in god's good time. Plautus, for better or worse, seems unconcerned about what happens to any of his characters as long as they provide a laugh or two on their way to the final curtain.

The Comedy of Errors is frequently dismissed as the most frivolous of Shakespeare's plays. It is taken as read that later comedies from *All's Well that Ends Well* to *As You Like It* have their thoughtful side. They also have their New Comedy characters, a braggart soldier in Parolles (is not Falstaff part of the same tradition?), a malcontent in Jacques. *The Comedy of Errors* contains, I would maintain, a similar seriousness of purpose to the later plays through comedy. The genesis for such does seem to reside with Menander. What Menander offered for the first time, part of his true gift to

Western drama, was a concealed depth to characters who were outlined through their mask types. With so few plays and hence so little direct evidence, this must remain unproven, but it is speculation that may lead us, when such a line of argument is taken to its conclusion, to a different view of his legacy.

Shakespeare does not appear to see the family as a comic inspiration. Apart from the Gobbos in *The Merchant of Venice*, it is difficult to think of any father and son whose relationship is treated less than seriously. For Menander this is the wellspring. Although too few plays of Menander survive to generalize, it rather seems that for him *only* family relationships are to be taken seriously. Perhaps it appears so because of the limited range of encounters that Athenian social life and Menander's reaction to it permit. Outsiders, especially cooks whose ubiquity can only be the product of their single-mindedness and their tendency to be needed on special occasions, have self-contained lives, touched but unaffected by all that goes on round them.

Beyond Shakespeare and into the English comedy tradition, Menander seems to have few immediate heirs. Jonson is too luscious in language, too full of guile and the gullible. The Restoration is too lubricious, with too much of a gleam in its eye. Menander's characters may not offer too much above the neck, but they do suggest there is something other than below the waist. Sentimental comedy glimmers rather than gleams and is simply too feeble for the heart-felt emotions that threaten to overwhelm Menander's people. With Sheridan, we come closer, notably in *The Rivals* where, suitably, the focus is again on the relationship of father and son.

Sheridan's relish for words and turns of phrase places him high in the hierarchy of Irish playwrights hijacked by the English stage. Wilde and Shaw are up there too, of course, but comparisons between them and Menander have fatal flaws. *The Rivals* may look forward to *The Importance of Being Earnest* in Lydia Languish's absurd prescription for a suitor, every bit as daft as Gwendolen's demand for a man called Ernest when the one she really wants is actually called Jack. *The Importance* looks back to a world of foundlings, recognition tokens, and miraculous revelations, but there any resemblance between Wilde and Menander founders. When a Menander character comes out with an aphorism, it is born of the character and the situation. Wilde simply shows he has just thought up a witty paradox. This is not to say that there are not scenes in *The Importance* as funny as any in stage comedy, but they are set pieces and essentially heartless.

The same is true of Shaw whose capacity to manipulate his characters does have a Menandrian hue. The difference in his case is the politics and the philosophy which tend to make of his people mouthpieces for the author. Actors playing Shaw soon discover he regularly writes longer lines than other playwrights. To speak them it is necessary to find the keyword and travel through the rest of the sentence. Done well, the technique is superbly comic, but it removes a whole layer of personality. This is, if anything, a return to the time when characters did not speak as individuals but were all the playwright's pawns.

In *The Rivals* Sheridan individualizes throughout. There are the broadly comic and largely stock figures of Mrs. Malaprop and Sir Lucius O'Trigger. There is also a father/son relationship that offers the closest of parallels to that of Demeas and Moschion in *The Woman from Samos*. Sir Anthony Absolute is determined to arrange a marriage between his son Captain Absolute and Lydia Languish. Lydia Languish and Captain Absolute are already in love, but because of her determination to marry someone insignificant, she knows him only as Ensign Beverley. This is a refinement impossible under Athenian social convention but a handy plot device in eighteenth-century Bath. When young Absolute hears his father wants to arrange his marriage, being in love already, he naturally wishes to hear who his future wife is to be:

SIR ANTHONY: What's that to you, sir? Come, give me your promise to love, and to marry her directly.

ABSOLUTE: Sure, sir, this is not very reasonable, to summon my affections for a lady I know nothing of!

SIR ANTHONY: I am sure, sir, it is more unreasonable in you to object to a lady you know nothing of. (*The Rivals* Act II, scene 1).

The expected row ensues with Sir Anthony exclaiming with all the self-righteous fury of a Menander father: "Can't you be cool, like me? What the devil good can passion do? Passion is no service, you impudent, insolent, overbearing reprobate!" No sooner does Captain Absolute discover that his father's choice happens to be his own anyway than he immediately plays hard to get. Part of his reason is to try to get around the double identity he has foisted on himself, but much more is precisely the same kind of pique that Moschion displays in Act Five of *The Woman from Samos* when he pretends he is going off to fight in the wars in order to punish his father for imagining him capable of making love to Chrysis.

The role of the servants is of interest here. The subworld of the Greek slave offered a number of refinements including the possibility of pursuing a profession outside the home. In Menander the slaves have a more prominent role than merely servicing the action. They are expected to be loyal, hard-working, and tactful: frequently, though not always, they prove the reverse. What they seldom have is responsibility. Sander M. Goldberg in his admirable investigation of the surviving plays[11] pointed to the way in which Plautus made the figure of the crafty slave the true "controller of the action." As Goldberg indicates, there is no evidence of a similar driving slave in Menander. Running slaves there are, hard-done-by slaves, clever slaves, grumbling slaves, but no one to compare with Plautus' Pseudolus.

In *The Malcontent* Pyrrhias, Daos, Simiche, and Getas serve between them the three families involved in the plot. Only one could be said to affect anything very much beyond relating what is going on outside the audience's view or informing their masters—as in Daos' case—of something suspicious he has seen. The exception is Getas who not only gets through his and the others' share of standard slave complaints, but in the last act takes the initiative in the revenge on Knemon.

Parmenon in *The Woman from Samos* has a far more pronounced function, cajoling Moschion, for whom he has a genuine concern, and providing comic drive by being at everyone's beck and call. He appears in four acts out of five and, as a conspirator in the initial plot to make Demeas think that the baby belongs to Chrysis, he finds himself everybody's target. His resumé in Act Five of what has happened and how he is in no way to blame is a fine distillation of all slaves in all comedies:

> And what crime have I committed? Let us investigate, point by point. One. The boy Moschion does what he shouldn't with a free girl. You can't blame Parmenon for that. She gets pregnant. Not guilty. The baby comes into our house. He brought it, not me. A member of the household claims it as hers. What did Parmenon do wrong? Nothing. So why did you run off, you silly coward? It's grotesque. He threatened to mark me for life. Yes, that's what it boils down to. It makes no odds whether you're in the right or not. One way or another, not very pleasant. (644–56)

Shakespeare's servants tend to be more put-upon than putting, though by the time of Molière and, especially, Beaumarchais, they will subvert their superiors with gusto. In *The Rivals* Sheridan has Fag and a Coachman introduce the play's intrigue as part of backstairs gossip. This enlivens the action by revealing a knowing class whose philosophy is admitted by Fag: "I beg pardon, sir—I beg pardon. But with submission, a lie is nothing unless one supports it. Sir, whenever I draw on my invention for a good current lie, I always forge endorsements as well as the bill" (Act II, scene 1). Fag serves as informant and adviser to Captain Absolute, both roles for trusted slaves in Menander. One last curiosity in *The Rivals* is an archetypal "running slave" who ups the tempo at the conclusion of the penultimate scene.

We can state with absolute confidence that Sheridan never read a play of Menander.[12] He may never even have heard of him. Such parallels that may be drawn between any plays of the seventeenth, eighteenth, and nineteenth centuries are incidental, if not accidental, and do no more than point to Menander's precocity.

The only exceptions might be Molière, or, at a pinch, Goldoni. Molière's early grounding in the *commedia* tradition was to give way to a substitution of the real mask for the social mask. He portrayed in plays such as *The Misanthrope* (1666), *The Miser* (1668), *The Bourgeois Gentleman* (1670), and *The Imaginary Invalid*, the play in which he performed on the night of his death in 1673, obsessives whose tortured world was barely comic. A capacity for seeing the world through his characters' eyes and the offer of at least token sympathy for the self-torturers raise one clear parallel to a Menander protagonist.

Knemon in *The Malcontent* is a misguided man in self-imposed exile from joy. The comparison to Molière's Alceste is interesting and surprising. Molière's celebrated misanthrope is a different sort of man.[13] Alceste is young, priggish, and terminally in love, all of which removes the play from any direct comparison with Menander's. What he does share with Knemon is a puritan disgust for the world.

"I hate all mankind," claims Alceste, "some because they are wicked and perverse, others because they tolerate wickedness." He rails against fashion, familiarity and hypocrisy, all legitimate enough targets, but is too convinced of his own righteousness to be taken for a reliable preacher. "My love is beyond all imagining," he tells Celimène. "No man has ever loved the way I do." By the last act when Alceste declares that "men ought to be other than they are," it is less the despairing cry of a frustrated moralist than an excuse for self-imposed banishment from society.

Knemon's fate is different. In rejecting the world Knemon treats life as an ordeal to get through, but one that he would prefer to cope with by himself. He has no wish to invite anyone else to share his world and is reconciled to losing his daughter. What happens to him proves he cannot live in total isolation but it does not convert him. Here Menander and Molière overlap. The final scene in which Knemon is pressganged into joining the party offers scant hope of a change of heart. Molière was as suspicious as Menander of the happy ending.

A major achievement of Molière's was to liberate himself from the stranglehold of Aristotelian regulation which French academicism had imposed on the rest of their serious drama. Beaumarchais, whose *Barber of Seville* was first seen at the Comédie-Francaise in the same year as *The Rivals* reached Covent Garden, was to move classical comedy on to a sharper and more direct critique of a society about to undergo the most drastic of transformations. There is no Menander here.

The Italian comic tradition had revived in the sixteenth century through the *commedia erudita*, a form more consciously based on the Roman plays of Plautus and Terence. Ariosto, Cecchi, and Machiavelli, at least as a playwright, are now barely known. *Commedia dell'arte* survived longer and spread its influence throughout Europe. In decline by the beginning of the eighteenth century, the *commedia* encountered two reformers, Carlo Gozzi and Carlo Goldoni. While Gozzi attempted to breathe new life into the old forms, Goldoni abandoned improvisation in favor of fully scripted pieces. Interestingly, the most celebrated revivals of his best known play, *The Servant of Two Masters*, were several productions by Giorgio Strehler with the Piccolo Theatre of Milan from 1947 onward in *commedia* style as though played by a company of masked *commedia* actors.

Goldoni left at his death some one hundred and fifty plays. The sheer volume is impressive and suggests at the very least a technical precision. Such a prolific output does not guarantee profundity, but the few plays that still see the light of day such as *The Fan* and *The Boors* seem more to preserve the Italian tradition of local comedy than hint at some underestimated link to Greek New Comedy.

If the earlier analysis holds water, the nineteenth century appears to show that the ghost of Menander is standing at the elbow, not of the boulevardier, nor the writer of burlesque whose days have now arrived in England and France, but of a quite different dramatic novelty, allied more to the world of the novel of manners.[14]

Ivan Turgenev was thirty-seven when, in the autumn of 1856, he invented the Portrait Game. He had already spent thirteen years of his life entrenched as part of the entourage surrounding Pauline Viardot-Garcia and her husband Louis. Platonic though his relationship with Pauline was always to be, he remained attached to her for the rest of his life, dying in her arms in 1883. The Viardots were international celebrities, or at least Pauline was, renowned as a leading prima donna of her day. It was at the Chateau de Courtavenel, her country home in Seine-et-Marne, that Turgenev first conceived the idea of drawing sketches, portraits of imaginary people, for the rest of the guests to analyze.

Here were pinned down like butterflies in a case "a retainer, elderly from the hour of his birth—good but easily inveigled into doing things of doubtful probity"; "a swashbuckler—cavalry officer—courageous, vindictive—no tenderness"; "a young man from a wealthy family, passionately addicted to hunting and shooting"; and a whole host of more or less stock characters, the sort about whom Turgenev wrote his sketches and stories: pen sketches, it might be suggested, equivalent in nineteenth-century Europe to Theophrastus' *Characters* in late fourth-century Athens.

Few of Turgenev's plays are known outside Russia, the major exception being *A Month in the Country*, "scenes from country life." The play is celebrated as the first psychological drama. Chekhov claimed not to be remotely influenced by it but allowed the writer Trigorin in *The Seagull* to suggest as his own epitaph: "Here lies Trigorin. He was a good writer: but not as good as Turgenev."

In proposing Menander as the founder of a generalized European comic tradition, the elements of his plays most frequently invoked, as we have seen, are those that inspired his Roman borrowers. From there the *commedia dell'arte* with its mask types and its restricted range of subjects led in due time to Molière and his range of obsessive "masks." From Molière, however, the genealogy becomes patchy with some exploration of new refinements in high and sentimental comedy, from Farquhar through to Sheridan. Conjuring the names of Turgenev and Chekhov, however, is less far-fetched than it might at first appear. Behind the masks of Menander; beneath the surface dialogue; and beyond the limited social framework, lies a kind of family comedy which is very much the stuff of Chekhov and Turgenev. Families tend to communicate in shorthand, as Coward so brilliantly exposed in *Hayfever*. Chekhov was the first fully to explore the subtextual qualities of such shorthand to reveal how often people will mean something different from what they are saying.

The characters of Aristophanes are supremely direct. No one says one thing to save hurting another's feelings while meaning something else. His is a world of "brash winds" where anything more delicate than appetite is swiftly put in its place by a kick up the arse.

The tragic writers knew more about dissembling, Euripides in particular, who can frequently use duplicity as a shock tactic. The first surviving play, *Alkestis*, as we saw in Chapter 2, revolves around a man who has to come to terms with his decision to allow his wife to die instead of him. Admetus' capacity for self-deception is severely strained when challenged first by his father, Pheres, and then his friend Herakles whom he receives into his house as a guest, while maintaining the fiction that the death in the household is that of a distant relative. This may be the first use in drama of what T. G. Rosenmeyer described as "the art of glancing speech."[15] Menander, as we have seen, learned from Euripides. As in all aspects of his art, he borrowed and created anew.

A practicing doctor who wrote stories of the horrors of peasant existence and human fallibility, Chekhov is better known as one of the world's few great playwrights. His major plays were concentrated into the last eight years of his life, on either side of the turn of the nineteenth century into the twentieth. In them there is no evidence of the Jewish pogroms in Moscow nor of the factional ferment that led to the foundation of the Bolshevik party. There is plenty of talk, but Trophimov, the only paper revolutionary, never gets near a barricade. The soldiers never have to fight, and what deaths do occur become ever more distant. The effete gentry may be dispossessed by the gentle revolution of bourgeois pragmatism, but the nearest to dangerous disruption in the lives of his characters comes with the brief entrance of a threatening itinerant in Act Two of *The Cherry Orchard*.

Yet Chekhov's sheer parochialism bestows universality by bringing all issues to the level of social grouping. Tied so firmly to the *fin de siècle*, "the voice of twilight Russia," as Princess Toumanova entitled her biography of him, Chekhov has that Menandrian quality of belonging to us all. The closer we look at Menander's plays, the more subtle the major relationships appear, never as deep and complex as in Chekhov's diminishing perspective, but dense and varied despite their restricted range.

As in Chekhov, there appear to be few villains in Menander. People may be greedy, calculating, and self-centered, but malice is uncommon and all the more striking when it does rear its head. Melodrama makes taking sides easy by underlining the virtues and vices of the characters three times in red. Chekhov allows you to take to some characters rather than others, but he always leaves the actor the option of seeing the world from the character's point of view.

Where next? The twentieth century can boast such an outpouring of drama in every direction and in every country that the possibilities seem endless. Equally they seem finite. Serious drama has developed in waves. Naturalism was superseded by symbolism, symbolism by expressionism, expressionism by dadaism and surrealism on the one hand, socialist realism on the other: we have had theatre of the mass, poetic theatre, political theatre, theatre of the absurd: we have had fantasy, musical theatre, dance theatre, feminst theatre, constructivist theatre and deconstructionist theatre, modernism, post-modernism, theatre that looks back, theatre that looks forward, theatre whose sole message is that theatre is dead. None of it owes anything to Menander.

A number of comic writers from Pinero on have kept alive a realistic family-rooted tradition. Moss Hart, Somerset Maugham, Neil Simon, and Alan Bennett have all proved that the source is unlikely ever to dry up. Menander might have been proud to have written Noel Coward's *Hayfever* or Mary Chase's *Harvey*. Alan Ayckbourn has kept up a Menandrian pace with a play a year since the late 1960s; many of them are comedies Menander might have recognized, about middle-class people teetering on the edge of despair.

Menander, however, is too slender a trunk to bear such a weight of branches, and it is unfair to force him to do so. His plays, such as they are, do offer a number of points of comparison to the comedy of later time without necessarily having affected it directly. The patterns of contrast, for example, between rich and poor, city-bred and rustic, free man and slave, young and old, women and men are the same as can be found in all comedy, high and low, from the broadest *commedia* scenario to the Broadway comic scene.

If one is genuinely seeking Menander's children, they are probably lurking behind a screen. The emphasis on the quirks and vicissitudes of family life became a weekly diet with the growth of Hollywood, an hourly one with the arrival of television into every home in the land. Where would the television situation comedy or soap opera be without the twin gods of Chance and Ignorance, the generation gap, and the battles of the sexes?

How unfair! Menander falls asleep like Mayakovsky's Prisypkin or Woody Allen's "Sleeper" and wakes up as the father of Roseanne. No. Let us simply acknowledge that in the last twenty-two years of the fourth and the first eight of the third centuries B.C. a prolific playwright wrote pleasing and truthful comedies about day-to-day affairs. Reasonably successful during his life, his plays became more so after his death for their common sense and their humanity. If, thereafter, they influenced other writers, other playwrights, that is their business or the business of theatre historians. They may have inspired a comic dynasty, but they are just as interesting for the light they throw on a lost way of life.

Slavery, legalized prostitution, arranged marriage: by twentieth-century standards, it was hardly a promising life for the majority living in Menander's Athens. What we do see from his plays is some sense of a society that was ordered in its own lights: a society, moreover, in which it was possible to examine fundamental relationships, particularly family ones. Here his comedies do bridge the centuries without the need for any intervention by subsequent dramatists. The feelings of Menander's characters have the capacity to raise a smile and touch the heart. It is the sympathy here engaged and the awareness of human frailty which confirm Menander as the founder of dramatic humanism.

NOTES

1. E. W. Handley, *Menander and Plautus: A Study in Comparison*, London: Lewis, 1968.
2. N. Miller, *Menander: Plays and Fragments*, Harmondsworth: Penguin, 1987.
3. *On the Razzle* based on Nestroy's *Einen Jux will er sich machen*; *Rough Crossing* adapted from Molnar's *Play at the Castle*; and *Undiscovered Country*, a version of Schnitzler's *Das weite Land*.
4. See p. 33.
5. Plautus' full name was Titus Maccius Plautus.
6. The history of the *commedia dell'arte* is charted in several books including P. L. Duchartre, *The Italian Comedy*, London: Harrop, 1929 and G. Oreglia, *The Commedia dell' Arte*, London: Methuen, 1968.
7. Wiles, *The Masks of Menander*, Cambridge: Cambridge University Press, 1952, pp. 121–28 and 140–49.
8. G. E. Duckworth, *The Nature of Roman Comedy*, Princeton, N.J.: Princeton University Press, 1952. Chapter 15 is devoted to the influence of Plautus and Terence on English comedy.
9. Peter Brook, *The Empty Space*, London: Macgibbon and Kee, 1968, Chapter 3.
10. Peter D. Arnott, *The Birds and the Brothers Menaechmus*, New York: Appleton-Century-Crofts, 1958, p. xi.
11. S. M. Goldberg, *The Making of Menander's Comedy*, London: Athlone Press, 1980.
12. Nonetheless, Norma Miller performed an important service when she drew together a number of critical reviews: "the reversals spring from characterisation"; "the struggle between father and son is presented with rueful humour"; "When the language takes a highly literary flow, the reason is often to be found in the self-importance of the speaker": and pointed out that they were all from an Introduction to Sheridan, not Menander. Miller, *Menander: Plays and Fragments*, Introduction, p. 10.
13. A main reason for my translating *Duskolos* as *The Malcontent*.
14. Peter Green who is so derisive of Menander in his *Alexander to Actium*, Los Angeles: University of California Press, 1990, pp. 65–79, does invoke the name of Jane Austen but only negatively. The most he will allow is "a mood both genteel and escapist," a poor substitute, he claims, for the "free spirit" of Aristo-

phanes. Fifteen pages devoted to Theophrastus and Menander in a book of nearly a thousand necessarily makes for a superficial analysis.

15. T. G. Rosenmeyer, *Drama*, in M. I. Finley (ed.), *The Legacy of Ancient Greece*, Oxford: Oxford University Press, 1983, p. 125.

Appendix 1

A Summary of Plutarch's Comparison between Aristophanes and Menander

The following is my translation of an essay appended to the manuscript of Book Ten of Plutarch's *Moralia* (853–54) and probably written by the compiler from a fuller essay by Plutarch himself.

For the most part, he (Plutarch) infinitely prefers Menander, especially when he offers the following comments:

"Coarse language, theatrical and tradesmen's talk are a feature of Aristophanes but never of Menander. The uneducated and the commoner will be delighted by what Aristophanes has to say, but not the man of refinement: I am referring to antitheses, rhymes and puns. Menander does use this sort of wordplay but sparingly, deeming such things devices to be employed with caution. Not so Aristophanes who uses them all the time, inappropriately and pointlessly. He wins applause for 'drenching bankers like tankers': or 'blowing a north wind and an ill wind. . . .' (there follows a selection of untranslateable and somewhat unwieldy examples of word-play).

And his language includes the tragic, the comic, the pompous, the pedestrian, the obscure, the mundane, the inflated, the elevated, the gossipy and all manner of sickening rubbish. And with all this variety he cannot manage to get the appropriate differences of speech for the right people: dignity for a king, eloquence for an orator, shrewdness for a woman, common speech for a common man, slang for the streetwise. He doles out whatever language turns up to any character as though handing it out by lot. There is no way of telling whether someone is a father or a son from what they say, a yokel or a god, an old woman or a hero.

Menander's diction, on the other hand, is so smooth and consistent that he manages to adapt it to the whole range of emotions, personalities and character traits: and that, while harmonising the whole and employing words that are in everyday use. If the action calls for something out of the ordinary or brash, he can still 'pull out the stops,' so to speak, and just as quickly return to normal. You get fine craftsmen of all sorts but never a shoemaker, a maskmaker or costumier to make a shoe, a mask or a costume the same for a man and a woman, the young, the old or the slave. Menander, though, managed to use language appropriate to any temperament, condition or age: and he did so though he was still young when he entered the profession and was still in his prime as a playwright when he died, a time when, according to Aristotle, the writer most cultivates his style. Were we to compare early Menander with the middle and late plays, we might get some impression of how far he could have progressed, had he lived.

It is obvious that some playwrights write for mass appeal, others for the minority. Not many can adapt to satisfy everyone. Aristophanes was unable to please the majority while to men of judgement he was intolerable. He writes like a superannuated whore taking on wifely airs with a brashness which most people would find unacceptable and a vulgarity that decent folk would spurn. Menander, though, along with his other virtues, was unique. Of all the poetry produced in Greece, in the theatre, in schools, on social occasions, Menander's outranks the rest in performance, as a textbook or in private readings. He demonstrates true refinement of speech, dealing with any subject with unassailable conviction: he is a master of the sound and nuance of the Greek language. Why, if the truth be told, should any man of education ever go to the theatre except for Menander? When else do you see a cultured audience for a comedy? Or menu and wine-list take second place at a symposium? When painters need to relax, they turn to the colours of flowers and grass. Men of intellect and education find Menander a source of recreation from intense study, a writer to beguile the mind, you might say, with light and shade, flowers and breezes.

The city has come up with any number of accomplished actors of comedy in recent times . . . (hiatus here: sc. 'but no playwright to match Menander') whose plays are witty and as salt as the sea from which Aphrodite was born. Aristophanes' jokes are bitter and prickly, with a sharp-edged cruelty about them. As for his so-called brilliance, I have no idea whether this is meant to be to do with language or character. His stage representations are always for the worse. He treats industriousness as malicious rather than the mark of a citizen; country values not as simplicity but something laughable, a subject for mockery; love is never joyful, simply coarse. The man seems to have written nothing for anyone decent, but vile and vulgar stuff for the crude-minded, slanderous and blasphemous for the spiteful and vicious."

Appendix 2

Speaking of the Play

This is a program note by Peter Arnott for his production of *The Man Who Hated People* (*Duskolos*), which opened at the Tufts Arena Theater on February 27, 1990.

Present last summer when Governor Dukakis opened an exhibition of Greek art at the MFA, I heard him say: "If you are born Greek, and have never been to Greece, when you finally get there, it is the most experience of your life." No, this is not a typo, but exactly what he said; and like several around me, I assumed that this was a case of a busy politician misreading a prepared script, and wondered what the missing adjective might be. And then it dawned upon me that no adjective is necessary. Greece is the most experience of your life; and you don't have to be born Greek to discover this.

Menander wrote a play which is, on the surface, a study of an old, rustic curmudgeon being given a new lease of life by contact with young love and warm humanity. But it's also a play about urban sophisticates, brash, spoilt, selfish, being purged by their contact with the country. Yes, Greece in the fourth century B.C. was already suffering from urban blight. For the present revival, we have chosen to extend the metaphor, and offer you a group of young worldlings wooed by the charms of a simpler and still pastoral way of life: the New World absorbing the lessons of the Old, with perhaps some trade-off in the opposite direction. So, laugh; enjoy; and have the most time of your life.

Appendix 3

Famous Lost Words

This pre-production article by Peter Arnott appeared in *Prologue* (Vol. 45, no. 3) for February 1990.

As the commentary on a later page will show, Menander's *Duskolos* (here translated as *The Man Who Hated People*) is one of the great rediscoveries of our time. I would not dare to boast that our production is an American première. Such a statement would immediately provoke angry letters from such places as the East Overshoe Business Secretarial and Cosmetology College claiming that they did it ten years ago. But there have not been many productions in English—or in any language, for that matter.

This rediscovery of a long-lost work prompts speculation about how much else is hidden out there, plays that we would long to have. The most famous gaps, of course, are classical, dating from a time when written scripts were few, and papyrus perishable. For the Greeks, the wishlist is easy: anything by anybody else, so that we might have some standard of comparison other than the tragic triad. If we could only read, for example, some of the works that beat the now-acknowledged masters in the festivals; or a comedy by one of Aristophanes' rivals, so that we could judge for ourselves whether he is as clever, and as different, as he claims to be.

For the Romans, it's easier. The surviving fragments of Roman tragedy are so appallingly dull that we may render thanks to Time for depriving us of the rest. We have enough Plautus; any more would simply confirm our estimate of him as a solid craftsman. And we already have far too much Terence. But there is one great absence, perhaps the most famous lost play of antiquity: Ovid's *Medea*. We have only the faintest hints of this work, but from the way the author treats the story in his nondramatic poems, we might reasonably expect a play lush, warm, emotional, and romantic years before its time, which would belie the standard vision of the Romans as stern and upright moralists given to weighty pronouncements in Ciceronian Latin; which would, in short, be as different from the rest of ancient tragedy as the Pompeian frescoes from the Parthenon.

For the middle ages, please, Santa, some more secular material, to pad out the few French examples that we have. Were they all so heartlessly materialistic as *The Blind Man and the Beggar*? And how, if at all, did they feed into the developing French tradition? For the Elizabethans, more of anything. A new play by Middleton turned up only a few years ago. And let us not forget the flurry caused by the emergence of a hitherto unknown poem, by, well, possibly, Shakespeare, discovered by a researcher who was simply sifting through the Shakespeare entries in the library's card catalog. For Molière some of the early farces, lost in the legendary trunk which went missing on a provincial tour.

And here we had better stop, for we have entered the period when plays began to be preserved *ad nauseam*; when they have always been there, and owe their rediscovery merely to some scholar who is desperate for a topic for his Ph.D. dissertation. Let us spare a thought for those famous, tantalizing works which are lost because they never happened. Verdi's *King Lear*, for instance, which would have been the climax of his operatic versions of Shakespeare, crowning a list which already contained *Macbeth*, *Othello* and *Falstaff*. But he died before he wrote it. Or, in a lighter mood, *Alice in Wonderland* as an operetta, with music by—yes, you've guessed it—Gilbert and Sullivan. It was discussed by management, but never came to pass. If only it had.

The theme of the famous lost work has permeated recent fiction. Umberto Eco's *The Name of the Rose* turns on the world's last copy of Aristotle on comedy, destroyed by fire in a medieval scriptorium. Other works have offered a hitherto unknown novel by the Brontë sisters and the manuscript of Beethoven's Tenth Symphony. The last has, in a strange, roundabout and partial way, almost come true; and the rediscovery of Menander on mummy wrappings, which sounds like the most melodramatic of fictions, has in fact come true.

But let us turn the tables. Which of the works we now possess would we be glad to see lost? All of us in the theatre, I think, have a list of plays we never want to see again. My own private list is headed by Beckett's *Endgame*. It goes on to include *Hamlet*. George Bernard Shaw, years ago, suggested that there should be a moratorium on certain Shakespeare revivals. It might be timely to revive this suggestion now.

Appendix 4

Menander at the Getty

J. Michael Walton

The J. Paul Getty Museum in Malibu is a reconstruction of the Roman Villa dei Papiri at Herculaneum buried at the time of the eruption of Mount Vesuvius in 79 A.D. Opened in 1974, though never visited by its founder, the Museum is home to a collection of works of art and artifacts, many of which are from the Greek and Roman periods.

In 1993 Barbara and Lawrence Fleischman invited the Museum to select some 250 items from their private collection for a major Exhibition at the Getty to be entitled *A Passion for Antiquities*. The Exhibition would stay for four months in California before moving on to the Cleveland Museum.

As several of the vases and statuettes had theatrical connections and, as they were themselves keen theatre-goers, the Fleischmans suggested that it might be appropriate to stage a production at the Museum to coincide with the opening of the Exhibition in October 1994. Eventually it was decided to present a full professional production in conjunction with UCLA and the Mark Taper Forum of Los Angeles of two New Comedies, one Greek, one Roman, in the Inner Peristyle gardens.

The plays chosen were Menander's *The Woman from Samos*, in my translation which Methuen had published the previous March, and Plautus' *Casina*, translated by Richard Beacham. Both plays were to be performed with the same cast on Beacham's replica Plautine stage, based on his reconstructions from paintings in the Room of the Masks at the House of Augustus in Rome and from several houses in or near Pompeii.[1] This stage was built in the workshops at UCLA where early rehearsals took place, before being installed in the Inner Peristyle gardens for performances throughout October, 1994.

The productions were directed by Michael Hackett with a highly experienced and professional cast and with Beacham and I acting as dramaturgs for our respective translations. A full assessment of the work on the Menander appears in *Drama*[2] but it is worth recording here that several of the hypotheses and suppositions posited in this book were tested in this performance. There was a double priority behind the productions: firstly, to provide a faithful rendition, as far as was possible, of these two widely contrasting plays, one from Hellenistic Greece, the other from a Republican Rome which borrowed much of its dramatic fare from the Greece of a hundred and more years earlier; secondly, to present full and living productions which would in every way satisfy a contemporary audience looking for a great deal more than some arcane academic exercise.

In such an exquisite setting and with the Getty's bust of Menander looking directly into the wings from his home in one of the galleries, these two priorities were, I believe, able to blend without too much being sacrificed to either. The results were received with such enthusiasm by the *Los Angeles Times* that their critic called for the creation of a permanent resident company devoted solely to performing the classics. Philhellenists and philanthropists, please take note.

In the present context, let me simply rehearse some of my own conclusions about *The Woman from Samos* and record that I went back to the text of this book to make a number of revisions in the light of what had been learnt in an exciting and enlightening six weeks of rehearsal. Most reassuring was how often academic and practical issues may turn out to be one and the same.

First and foremost the production showed that *The Woman from Samos* can play to a contemporary audience. A creative and inspired company uncovered a dramatic inventiveness which went a long way towards justifying Menander's reputation as both realist and theatre craftsman. No apology of any kind is necessary for demanding a place in the world's repertoire for a play of such ingenious and complex dramatic tempo.

Second, however based on a tradition of masked, and hence physical theatre, Menander's greatest innovation is clearly in subtle nuance. The initial problems that the actors had in rehearsal were keeping up with how much their character was meant to know or believe at any time, compared to that of the others on stage. It turned out possible to uncover, and I refuse to put this down to anachronistic interpretation, a complex subtext, a subtext which reveals true feelings despite, rather than because of, what the characters happen to be saying. There is also a subtext of action which revolves around what people think is going on compared with what the audience know is really going on.

Third, the actors discovered that the motives of their characters might be complex but were understandable and consistent. This legitimized the search for whole and realized personalities. It was possible to think of Demeas, Moschion and Chrysis as having a past and a future as well as a present.

In all of this, and in the mix of the comic and the serious, the analogy with Chekhov became more and more plausible. What we were working with was not latterday *commedia* with a few poignant moments but a social, if parochial, comedy in which personal crises may take place in the most absurd of contexts. The Getty production was, of course, modern actors working with a modern translation and in a wholly artificial setting. It still suggested that Menander's dramatic method, at least in *The Woman from Samos*, is to demonstrate how in life the serious can be overtaken by the ridiculous. This puts him in the forefront of a rather different comic tradition from that usually suggested.

NOTES

1. See Richard Beacham, *The Roman Theatre and Its Audience*, London: Routledge, 1991.

2. J. Michael Walton, "Realising Menander: Get-in at the Getty," *Drama*, Winter issue, 1996.

Chronology

510 Expulsion of Hippias from Athens

490 Battle of Marathon. Athenians defeat the Persians

480 Second invasion of Persians; Athenian victory at Salamis

470 Growth of Athenian democracy

449 Reconstruction of the Acropolis by Perikles including the development of the Precinct of Dionysus and the theatre

431 Outbreak of the Peloponnesian War against Sparta

429 Death of Perikles

415–13 Sicilian Expedition

406 Athenian victory at Arginusai

404 Athenian surrender to the Spartans

399 Execution of Sokrates

384 Birth of Aristotle

c.380 Plato's *The Republic*

c.370 Birth of Theophrastus

c.532 Introduction of Tragedy at the Great Dionysia in Athens

496 Birth of Sophocles

486 Comedy admitted to the Great Dionysia

?480 Birth of Euripides

456 Death of Aeschylus in Sicily

c.455 Euripides' first play

449 Prizes for actors at the Great Dionysia

c.445 Birth of Aristophanes

438 Euripides' *Alkestis*

433 Actor's prizes at the Lenaia Festival

427 Aristophanes' first play, *The Banqueters*, not extant

425 First surviving Old Comedy, Aristophanes' *Acharnians*

421–408 Euripides' *Ion*

412 Euripides' *Helen*

367 Aristotle joins the Academy

359 Philip assumes government of
     Macedon

347 Death of Plato

338 Greece defeated by Philip at
     Chaironeia

336 Death of Philip and accession of
     Alexander

335 Aristotle founds Lyceum

323 Death of Alexander

322 Battle of Krannon; Antipater
     rules in Athens; suicide of De-
     mosthenes; death of Aristotle

319 Death of Antipater and De-
     metrius of Phaleron becomes re-
     gent of Athens

c.317 Theophrastus' *Characters*

307 Replacement of Demetrius of
     Phaleron by Demetrius Poliorketes;
     Epicurus founds school in Athens

300 Zeno founds Stoic School in Ath-
     ens

297–272 Campaigns of Pyrrhus

214 The Macedonian wars

407 Euripides leaves Athens for
     Macedon

406 Death of Euripides and Sophocles

405 Aristophanes' *Frogs*

404 Athenians defeated in the
     Peloponnesian War by Sparta

c.400–c.323 Middle Comedy

392 Aristophanes' *Women in Power*

388 Aristophanes' *Wealth*

c.385 Death of Aristophanes

c.361 Birth of Philemon

c.342 Birth of Menander

c.330 Lykurgus reconstructs the Thea-
     tre of Dionysus in stone

323 New Comedy

?321 Menander's first play *Anger,*
     which has not survived

?317 *The Malcontent (Duskolos)*;
     ?Theophrastus' *Characters*

?c.305 *The Woman from Samos*
     (Samia)

c.300–290 Diphilus fl.

c.292 Death of Menander

c.288 Formation of the Actors' Guilds

c.254 Birth of Plautus

195 or 185 Birth of Terence

184 Death of Plautus

159 Death of Terence

Select Bibliography

Arnott, P. D. *Greek Scenic Conventions*. Oxford: Oxford University Press, 1962. Reprinted Westport, Conn.: Greenwood Press, 1979.

————. *Public and Performance in the Greek Theatre*. London: Routledge, 1989.

Arnott, W. G. *Menander, Plautus, Terence*. Oxford: Oxford University Press, 1975.

————. *Menander, Vol. I, Aspis to Epitrepontes*. London and Cambridge, Mass., Heinemann and Harvard University Press, 1979.

————. *Time, Plot and Character in Menander*. In Papers of the Liverpool Latin Seminar, Vol. 2, pp. 343–60. Liverpool: 1979.

Bain, D. (ed.) *Menander, Samia*. Warminster: Aris and Phillips, 1983.

Beacham, R. C. *The Roman Theatre and Its Audience*. London: Routledge, 1991.

Bernarbo-Brea, L. *Menandro e il Teatro Greco nelle Terracotte Liparesi*. Genoa: 1981.

Berthiaume, G. *Les Rôles du Mageiros*. Leiden: Brill, 1982.

Blundell, J. *Menander and the Monologue*. Gottingen: Vandenhoeck and Ruprecht, 1980.

Boughner, D. C. *The Braggart in Renaissance Comedy*. Westport, Conn.: Greenwood Press, 1954.

Bury, J. B. *The Hellenistic Age*. 2nd ed. Cambridge: Cambridge University Press, 1925.

Cameron, A., and Kuhrt, A. (eds.). *Images of Women in Antiquity*. London: Croom Helm., 1983.

Charitonidis, S., Kahil, L., and Ginouvès, R. *Les Mosaiques de la Maison du Ménandre à Mytilène*. Antike Kunst, Beiheft VI. Bernn: 1970.

Dover, K. J. *Greek Popular Morality in the Time of Plato and Aristotle*. Oxford: Blackwell, 1974.

Duchartre, P. L. *The Italian Comedy: The Improvisation, Scenarios, Lives, Attributes, Portraits and Masks of the Illustrious Characters of the commedia dell' arte*. London: Harrop, 1929.

Duckworth, G. E. *The Nature of Roman Comedy: A Study in Popular Entertainment*. Princeton, N.J.: Princeton University Press, 1952.

Easterling, P. E., and Knox, A.M.W. (eds.). *The Cambridge History of Classical Literature, Vol. 1*. Cambridge: Cambridge University Press, 1985.

Fantham, E. "Sex, Status and Survival in Hellenistic Athens: A Study of Women in New Comedy." In *Phoenix*, 29, 1975, pp. 44–74.

Finley, M. I. (ed.). *Slavery in Ancient Greece*. Cambridge: Cambridge University Press, 1960.

————— (ed.). *The Legacy of Ancient Greece*. Oxford: Oxford University Press, 1984.

Frost, K. B. *Exits and Entrances in Menander*. Oxford: Clarendon Press, 1988.

Goldberg, S. M. *The Making of Menander's Comedy*. London: Athlone Press, 1980.

Gomme, A. W., and Sandbach, F. H. *Menander, a Commentary*. Oxford: Oxford University Press, 1973.

Green, J. R. *Theatre in Ancient Greek Society*. London and New York: Routledge, 1994.

Green, P. *Alexander to Actium*. Los Angeles: University of California Press, 1990.

Handley, E. W. (ed.). *The Dyskolos of Menander*. London: Methuen, 1965.

—————. *Menander and Plautus: A Study in Comparison*. London: Lewis, 1968.

Henry, M. M. *Menander's Courtesans and the Greek Comic Tradition*. Frankfurt and New York: Lang, 1985.

Hunter, R.L. *The New Comedy of Greece and Rome*. Cambridge, Cambridge University Press, 1985.

Just, R. *Women in Athenian Law and Life*. London and New York: Routledge, 1989.

Katsouris, A. G. *Linguistic and Stylistic Characterization*: *Tragedy and Menander*. Ionannina: University of Ioannina, 1975.

—————. *Tragic Patterns in Menander*. Athens: Hellenic Society for Humanistic Studies, 1975.

Lacey, W. K. *The Family in Classical Greece*. London: Thames and Hudson, 1968.

Lefkowitz, M. R. *Women in Greek Myth*. Baltimore: John Hopkins University Press, 1986.

Lowe, N. J. "Tragic Space and Comic Timing in Menander's Dyskolos" in *Bulletin of the Institute of Classical Studies*, 34, 1987, pp. 126–38.

MacCary, W. T. "Menander's Slaves: Their Names, Roles and Masks. *Transactions of the American Philosophical Association*, 100, 1969, pp. 277–94.

————. "Menander's Characters: Their Names, Roles and Masks." *Transactions of the American Philosophical Association* 101, 1970, pp. 277–90.

————. "Menander's Old Men." *Transactions of the American Philosophical Association* 102, 1971, pp. 303–25.

————. "Menander's Soldiers: Their Names, Roles and Masks." *American Journal of Philology*, 93, 1972, pp. 279–98.

Magistrini, S. "Le descrizioni fisiche dei personaggi in Menandro, Plauto e Terenzio." *Dioniso*, 44, 1970, pp. 79–114.

Miller, N. (trans.). *Menander: Plays and Fragments.* Harmondsworth and New York: Penguin, 1987.

Mossé, C. (trans. J. Stewart). *Athens in Decline.* London and Boston: Routledge and Kegan Paul, 1973.

Oreglia, G. *The Commedia dell'Arte.* London: Methuen, 1968.

Peradotto, J., and Sullivan, J. P. (eds.). *Women in the Ancient World.* The Arethusa Papers. Albany: State University of New York Press, 1984.

Pickard-Cambridge, A. W. *The Theatre of Dionysus in Athens.* Oxford: Clarendon Press, 1946.

————. *The Dramatic Festivals of Athens.* 2nd ed. Revised by J. Gould and D. M. Lewis. Oxford: Clarendon Press, 1968.

Pollitt, J. J. *Art in the Hellenistic Age.* Cambridge: Cambridge University Press, 1988.

Post, L. A. "Woman's Place in Menander's Athens." *Transactions and Proceedings of the American Philological Association* 71, 1940, pp. 420–59.

Préaux, C. "Ménandre et la Société Athénienne." *Chronique d'Egypte*, 32, 1957, pp. 84–100.

Prosperi, M. "The Masks of Lipari," *The Drama Review* (T96) Vol. 26, no. 4, Winter 1982, pp. 25–36.

Rasmussen, T., and Spivey, N. *Looking at Greek Vases.* Cambridge: Cambridge University Press, 1991.

Sandbach, F. H. "Menander and the Three-Actor Rule." *Le Monde Grec: Hommages à Claire Préaux.* Brussels, University of Brussels, 1975. pp. 197–204.

————. *The Comic Theatre of Greece and Rome.* London: Chatto and Windus, 1977.

Shapiro, H. A. *Myth into Art.* London and New York: Routledge, 1994.

Sifakis, G. M. *Studies in the History of Hellenistic Drama.* London: Athlone Press, 1967.

Taplin, O. *Comic Angels.* Oxford: Oxford University Press, 1993.

Tarn, W., and Griffith, G. T. *Hellenistic Civilisation.* 3rd ed. London: Edward Arnold, 1952.

Turner, E. G. (ed.). *Ménandre.* Vol. XVI. Geneva: Fondation Hardt, 1970.

————. "Menander and the New Society of His Time." *Chronique d'Egypte*, 54, 1979, pp. 106–26.

Vince, R. W. *Ancient and Medieval Theatre: A Historiographical Handbook.* Westport, Conn.: Greenwood Press, 1984.

Walcot, P. *Greek Drama in Its Theatrical and Social Context.* Cardiff: University of Wales Press, 1976.

Wallbank, F. W. *The Hellenistic World.* Sussex and Atlantic Highlands, N.J.: Harvester and Humanities Press, 1981.

Walton, J. Michael. *Green Theatre Practice.* Westport, Conn.: Greenwood Press, 1980; and London: Methuen, 1991.

———.(ed. and trans. of Menander). *Aristophanes and Menander: New Comedy,* London: Methuen, 1994.

———. "Realising Menander: Get-in at the Getty." *Drama,* Winter 1996.

Webster, T.B.L. *Studies in Later Greek Comedy.* Manchester: Manchester University Press, 1953.

———. *Art and Literature in Fourth Century Athens.* London: Athlone Press, 1956.

———. *Studies in Menander.* 2nd ed. Manchester: Manchester University Press, 1960.

———. *Monuments Illustrating New Comedy.* Rev. ed. London: University of London Institute of Classical Studies, 1969.

———. *An Introduction to Menander.* Manchester and New York: Manchester University Press and Barnes and Noble, 1974.

Wiles, D. "Menander's Dyskolos and Demetrios of Phaleron's Dilemma." *Greece and Rome,* 31, 1984. pp. 170–180.

———. "Marriage and Prostitution in Classical New Comedy." *Themes in Drama,* 11, 1989, pp. 31–48.

———. *The Masks of Menander: Sign and Meaning in Greek and Roman Performance.* Cambridge: Cambridge University Press, 1991.

Index

About the Authors

J. MICHAEL WALTON is head of the Drama Department and Personal Professor at the University of Hull, United Kingdom. In addition to editing numerous works, he is author of *Greek Theatre Practice* (Greenwood, 1980), *The Greek Sense of Theatre: Tragedy Reviewed*, and *Living Greek Theatre: A Handbook of Classical Performance and Modern Production* (Greenwood, 1987). His translations have been performed in Britain and the United States, and include Menander's *The Woman from Samos*, produced at the Getty Museum in Malibu in 1994.

PETER D. ARNOTT was Professor of Dramatic Arts at Tufts University at the time of his death in 1990. In addition to lecturing, he regularly toured with a one-man marionette theatre performing plays from the classical repertoire. Among his publications are *An Introduction to the Greek World*, *An Introduction to the Greek Theatre*, *Greek Scenic Conventions in the Fifth Century B.C.*, *The Ancient Greek and Roman Theater*, *The Theatre in Its Time* and *Public and Performance in the Greek Theatre*. He also published translations from Greek, Latin, and French, many of which he directed in public productions.

ISBN 0-313-27216-6

90000>

EAN

9 780313 272165

HARDCOVER BAR CODE